# RETIRED FROM THE MILITARY
# REFUELED FOR THE MISSION

H. James Busch, Jr. – Andrea N. Busch

WriteHouse Publishing
Washington, DC

Copyright © 2014  H. James Busch, Jr. ~ Andrea N. Busch
PO Box 632 - Glenn Dale, MD 20769 ~ www.BeFamily2.com

WriteHouse Publishing

All rights reserved.

ISBN: 0692253947

ISBN-13: 978-0692253946

Cover Design: WriteHouse Publishing & LAN

# DEDICATION

We dedicate this book to our parents, Howard Busch, Sr., Patricia Joan (Meeks) Busch, and Neva B. Lloyd, who showed us a higher standard of life and living, although we never reached their peak it made us better parents than we could ever ask or think.

From James:
To my father who made knowing God easy because he was always there, working hard for his family, taking time to teach a son, strong to discipline when I was wrong, caring to comfort when I was undone, demonstrating true love for his wife, and protecting a family growing in life. Dad, I don't know what I would have done if you weren't there.

To my mother who overcame so many struggles and pains. She kept God as her first love and raised her family in Jesus' name. She epitomized the true sanctity of love and marriage, taught me how to recognize the presence of the Lord, and gave me the hunger and thirst to know Him more. She believed in me no matter what I was going through, and there was never a day when her children would be hungry when she cooked. She was the love of a mother and everything came from, "The Heart of Patricia." I truly miss you!

From Andrea:
To my mother Neva who has shown her love through her giving and doing. You are truly the wind beneath your children and your grandchildren's wings. The song, *Wind Beneath My Wings*, is so befitting to who you are and what you have given to me, your eldest daughter. *"You were content to let me shine,...that's your way mama. It might have appeared to go unnoticed, but I have got it all here in my heart. I want you to know I know the truth; I would be nothing without you."*

# ACKNOWLEDGMENTS

## (from Howard James Busch, Jr.)

I would like to acknowledge my Heavenly Father and the Lord Jesus Christ for giving me the meaning of life and the purpose of living. Thank you for providing the bridge to bring this sinful man to the calling of a son because of the Blood of Your Only Begotten One.

I acknowledge my wife, Andrea, she is feisty and loving and I adore my passionate woman that way. There has never been a dull moment in our life and it blesses me to have you as my wife. I love you more today than the first day I met you.

To my mother, Neva Lloyd: Thank you for taking the risk to give your daughter to this strange man who called you up to ask for her hand. I never knew in getting her I would get a mother who truly understands, the love of family and the power of Prayer and God's Word.

To my son, Joshua: Thank you for allowing me to be the father my father was to me.

To my daughter, Diamond: It can truly be said a man should never pursue a woman until he has the mind of a daughter's father.

To Bishop Carlton Pearson: You taught me true worship and ministry. You gave me the confidence to serve. I pray your rekindling to the Gospel of the Lord.

To all my family, people in life who I've touched and been touched by, whether for me or against me. You all helped shape me to become the person I am today, "More than a conqueror through Christ Jesus." Amen!

Finally, I want to acknowledge the beloved Dr. Nelson and Dr. Belcher with Build Forward Companies / WriteHouse Publishing who saw a tarnished gem and took the polish of God's anointing and brought back the luster and the glow. They believed the revitalized value of the gem should be shared with the world. This book is a result of their faith.

# CONTENTS

Our 7 Section **KINGDOM BLUEPRINT**　　　　　　　　　9

---

### SECTION 1
**Our Authority and Commander *is* the LORD JESUS CHRIST**

Chapter 1　　　　　　　　　　　　　　　　　　　13
Chapter 2　　　　　　　　　　　　　　　　　　　18
Chapter 3　　　　　　　　　　　　　　　　　　　21
Chapter 4　　　　　　　　　　　　　　　　　　　25

---

### SECTION 2
**Our Code of Conduct *is* the BIBLE**

Chapter 5　　　　　　　　　　　　　　　　　　　31
Chapter 6　　　　　　　　　　　　　　　　　　　33

---

### SECTION 3
**Our Duty *is* to LIVE for JESUS**

Chapter 7　　　　　　　　　　　　　　　　　　　45
Chapter 8　　　　　　　　　　　　　　　　　　　47
Chapter 9　　　　　　　　　　　　　　　　　　　51
Chapter 10　　　　　　　　　　　　　　　　　　　53

## SECTION 4
## Our Military Operation *is* the KINGDOM of GOD

| | |
|---|---:|
| Chapter 11 | 57 |
| Chapter 12 | 61 |

## SECTION 5
## Our Soldering Skills *are to* FIGHT the GOOD FIGHT of FAITH

| | |
|---|---:|
| Chapter 13 | 67 |
| Chapter 14 | 73 |

## SECTION 6
## Our Sacrifice *is* to DIE to SELF and LIVE for GOD

| | |
|---|---:|
| Chapter 15 | 81 |
| Chapter 16 | 89 |

## SECTION 7
## Our Mission *is* to MAKE DISCIPLES

A Closing Thought:
| | |
|---|---:|
| **D.R.I.V.E.** | 95 |
| **S.O.A.R.** | 107 |

| | |
|---|---:|
| **Military** Resources & References | 123 |
| **Spiritual** Resources & References | 142 |

The following 7 sections serve as a Kingdom Blueprint given to me by God through my Military service which has inspired my family's continued success.

## Through our faith we see life *is* Military Service:

1. **Our *Authority and Commander* *is* the LORD JESUS CHRIST.**

2. **Our *Code of Conduct* *is* the BIBLE.**

3. **Our *Duty* *is* to LIVE for JESUS.**

4. **Our *Military Operation* *is* the KINGDOM of GOD.**

5. **Our *Soldiering Skills* *are to* FIGHT the GOOD FIGHT of FAITH.**

6. **Our *Sacrifice* *is* to DIE to SELF and LIVE for GOD.**

7. **Our *Mission* *is* to MAKE DISCIPLES.**

# SECTION 1

# Our *Authority and Commander* is the LORD JESUS CHRIST

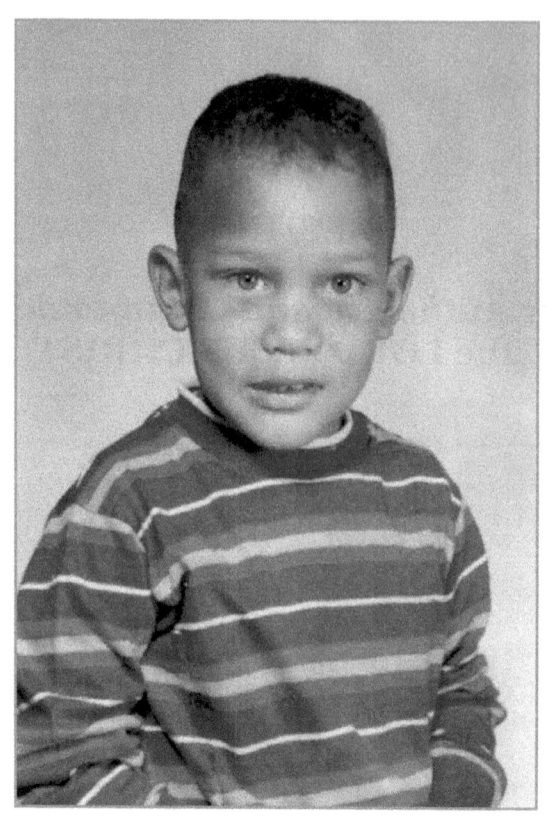

## **The Lessons I Learned While Serving In the Military**

### Chapter 1

I had basically made a mess of my life, my newly wedded wife left me after 6 months. (Justifiably but not biblically, I hadn't committed adultery. I'll talk about this later.) My ambition to become a medical doctor was in complete shambles. Serving in the military was the greatest fit for my life in 1983. It was while working door to door as an insurance salesman in Citrus Heights, California I came upon McClelland AFB, (*the same Base my father served on*), when I saw young airmen looking sharp and distinguished having a sense of connection and purpose. I heard myself say, "I wish I could be like them."

Two short months later, there I was standing on a platform at Lackland AFB in San Antonio, Texas late at night. It was quiet, until suddenly I heard the clicking sound of metal taps hitting the pavement surface and before my eyes there was what appeared to be a large and tall man. He had on a big cap, his uniform was impeccable and he began yelling in our faces. There wasn't enough space between his face and ours to stick a piece of paper. He was not alone; he brought several others with him male and female each exact replica's but different sizes. The thought went through my mind that I was in a scene of a movie, but this was very real.

I was in the Air Force now!

I like so many young men and women before me had to cross the same threshold, each having their own story and path as to what brought them to this moment in their lives. Throughout the entire United States there were young men and women like myself standing before drill sergeants in the Air Force, Army, Coast Guard, Marines, and Navy leaving civilian life to become one of the dedicated in serving their Country.

Thus began my military career, one that would shape me and make me into the man I am today. **"Bring me your tired and disposed**...I will make a real man and woman out of them." Having identified a qualified and tested skill on ASVAB[1], having passed the medical exam at MEPS[2], and having been screened for priors and drug use, this was a crucial step in my budding military record that qualified me to join the service. Although I had now begun the process of being called a service man I still did not have the full stamp of approval as there where many more phases for which I had to complete with a GO before I could be called a full service member.

The first lesson I learned as a service man was that no matter what I brought into the basic training camp it would all be placed in a closet and locked up. All that I was would now be stripped and taken away; every way that I saw myself, thought of myself and identified myself was being stripped away. All so that I could become what the military calls an airmen, coastie, marine, soldier, and sailor.

I would lose all my hair (and I had a lot *then*!)...

---

[1] ASVAB – The Armed Services Vocational Aptitude Battery is a multiple choice test, administered by the United States Military Entrance Processing Command, used to determine qualification for enlistment in the United States Armed Forces.

[2] MEPS – Military Entrance Processing Station.

I would lose all my clothes (whatever style I had developed)...

All that I was before this day of indoctrination was stripped so I could become a government issue; meaning everyone was identified by the same moniker – individuality ceased. My whole life of learning to be me was now reversed for the good of the whole.

I was provided a uniform...

I was told when to get up... When to eat, when to learn, and when to go to sleep. I was being tested in every way imaginable. This environment made sure my thoughts were insignificant as I even struggled to have a clear thought amidst the formidable rigidity I so willingly became a part of.

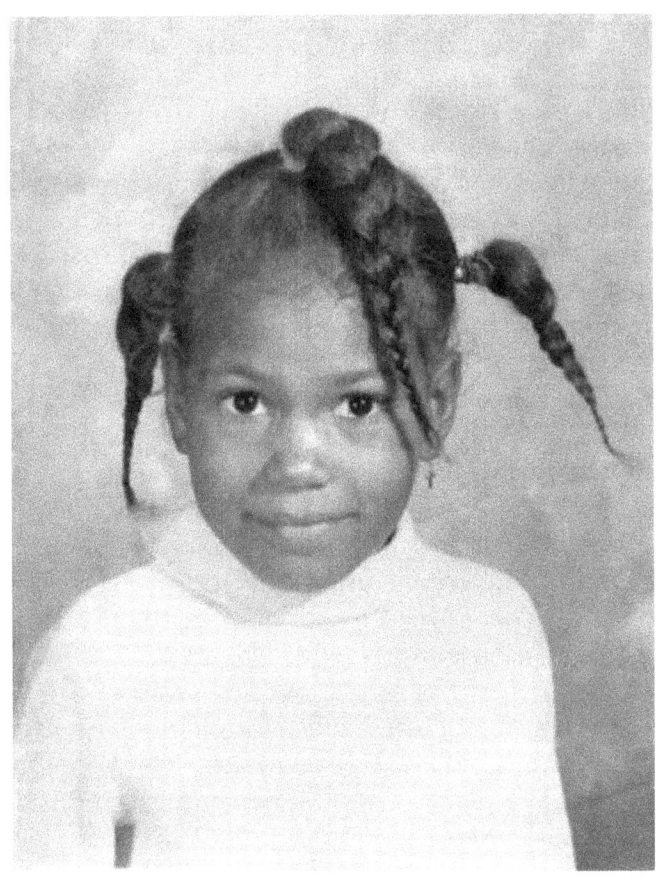

## **Humble Beginnings**

### Chapter 2

It's all here, I'm all in, allow me to share my story.

I am the wife of H. James Busch, Jr. of over 29 years, Andrea Nevoria Busch. I grew up outside of Wilmington, NC where I was born, in the little township/counties of Northwest and Riegelwood, NC. I was known as Angie (my nickname) Perkins. I am the eldest daughter to the marriage union of Oliver Thomas Perkins (aka O.T.) and Neva Bowens Perkins.

Life changed forever when James Busch came into my life but let me tell you *why* he is so significant to my humble beginnings and my life. I share with you my past to show you my future. The past is not my focus but rather the here and now. More specifically, what God has done and can do in any of our lives. I like what Bishop Don Meares shared early in 2013, **"This is not that!"** Referencing Deuteronomy 11:10, "For the land, where you go in to possess it, is not as the land of Egypt, from where you came out..."

Imperfect family, yes but special nonetheless. I still remember growing up in Northwest with so many amazing moments shared with my dad, my mom, and my sister Tammy. Even now, I'm remembering wonderful times of having aunts, uncles, and cousins all around me to grow up with. And that wasn't all; I had many more aunts, uncles, and cousins' not far away in Bladen County. Our community of close neighbors was family, one in which they all took part in raising you as a child; that was very special and something I will always cherish.

Our stories, events, happenings; life back then makes me smile when I think of them. In the country (referring to living outside the city where there is land and fields and farming) your next door neighbor could be over an acre away but you still felt close to your family. What is even more special was having our grandparents who were strong Christian pillars to the entire Perkins family. As a little girl I attended church at Perkinsville Baptist Church, founded by my grandfather, George Douglas Perkins. An honor I yet embrace today. I have lifelong memories of my Aunt Bernice Perkins Troy teaching us Sunday school in this little church. She was a Sunday school teacher in our church as well as a teacher in the Brunswick County School System but I was never in one of her classes during grade school. More than anything I remember Aunt Bernice for giving me the lessons of Jesus.

Yet, with this type of upbringing I had some extremely significant moments in my life, as a child, that created in me a *wanting for God* in my person beyond what I could just see with my eyes.

## The Lessons I Learned While Serving In the Military

Chapter 3

I discovered as a result of this new challenge that I was capable of a lot more than I had even thought or believed. I was selected to become the Dorm Chief, the recruit in charge of all the rest of the recruits. Titles always stroke your ego but the bottom line was if things did not get done it was my responsibility. Whatever the number of recruits in our dorm, every recruit had an assignment and regardless of any circumstance every one of us was expected without fail to fulfill that assignment. Which ultimately if that wasn't accomplished I had to answer to my superiors.

*For someone who never led anyone* this was a big bone to chew. I was afraid but that same fear was my motivator. I was not given a choice, it was decided, maybe because I was the older trainee, maybe because I had gone to college, but no matter what I was now the Dorm Chief. It was sink or swim.

I discovered that I could swim.

I discovered that I had a voice.

I discovered others would follow me as long as I knew where I was going.

I had to quickly learn where to go and how to get there. *It made me pay attention to life, something I had not fully done before* because up to this point I was only drifting. I discovered the *danger of drifting* immediately when I violated a rule. I attempted to go back to my old ways once while in the military dining facility. I saw a pretty female recruit, and attempted to talk to her, you know, put my old familiar rap on her but, *this new environment wasn't tolerating the old me.* I received immediate consequence for my action.

Like the quickest lightning flash that you almost didn't see, I was apprehended by a Drill Sergeant in the Pit (DS Table[3]), the slip of paper meticulously placed in my uniform pocket was pulled as an identifier of an offense. I had to see my Drill sergeant. Shock ran through me like an electric bolt. Fear gripped my mind.

Would I lose my Dorm Chief position?

Would I get kicked out of the service?

All because of my old ways.

When I was called in to my Drill Sergeants' office right away I could see the disappointment in his face. He said firmly, "What were you thinking about Basic Trainee Busch?" (Breaking me down). He continued, "I should take away your Dorm Chief status, but I believe in you. I am going to give you another chance, but don't let me down."

Words I was not familiar, "I believe in you." "I am going to give you a second chance."

I couldn't believe it; I had never been given a second chance at anything. That day forward I determined in my heart to never mess up like that again.

---

[3] DS Table – Drill Sergeant Table

I finally realized how our poor decisions impacted our life. With the military where behavior and actions could cause life or death it became clear that lapses in conduct could not be tolerated. Perhaps my Drill Sergeant could see that I had grasped the lesson; that is why he gave me another chance.

*I had to hold the standard*, to be the best.

## **Humble Beginnings**

### Chapter 4

It was Easter Sunday; I was all dressed up in my yellow dress with my yellow patent leather shoes (go on girl) and ready to give my Easter speech.

Easter speech, recitations, something we learned to do every year from the moment we could say, "Happy Easter Day." But on this particular Easter (Resurrection Sunday), someone (which I don't remember who but it could have been my Aunt Esther) was singing these words that began to pierce my heart: **"Were you there when they crucified my Lord? Were you there when they nailed him to the cross?"** I remember crying softly and fully in that moment as I heard those spirit-filled words.

My eyes were clouded with continuous tears from the deepening presence of the Lord. I felt him draw near; it was so real to me. Then…I heard his voice in my heart…God's voice so softly saying, *"I am and will be your father, I will take care of you."* What an incredible experience especially for an 8 year old!

I remember one of my cousins saying, "Why is she crying?" and I believe it was my wonderful Auntie Lucille that said, "She's crying because she misses her dad." But she wasn't aware, no, when I think about it no one was aware of the true transformation of that moment. It wasn't my dad I was crying about, (although I did have those times too), in that very moment I felt the unmistakable presence of God and His word spoken tenderly into my heart.

~ That was the day of my salvation ~

It was almost a year earlier that I watched my father alive; living in one moment and dead the next. It was again on a Sunday morning after church when my sister and I had come from Sunday school. He and my mom were preparing to go to East Arcadia, NC to visit my mother's mom, Grandma Pearl. They were going for a Sunday afternoon ride on his motorcycle. My dad was all dressed, sharp as usual, as he always liked to dress. My mom too was all ready to go. But wait there was a small interruption in their plans as they had a visitor, a cousin, from Baltimore.

The cousin, Douglas, Jr. came from just a short distance and across the way from my grandparents to see my dad. I don't remember all of their conversation but as usual I was close by. What I do remember is my dad was showing his cousin his motorcycles and mostly his latest big cycle. My dad really loved his motorcycles, I could see his delight every time he talked about them, worked on them, shined them up; those were his babies. His latest was huge to me, a beautiful burgundy motorcycle.

Cousin Douglas asked to ride it, so my dad let him. Douglas got on to ride and hadn't gone far out of the driveway before he turned the motorcycle over.

~ What followed changed my life forever ~

My father makes a mad dash over to him and immediately picks up the motorcycle. He looks at his cycle to see if it's okay and then, jumps on it. I can see and hear Cousin Douglas asking if he could ride with him.

And with a stern look in his face, my father says, "No!" He proceeds to pull out of the driveway and down pass our house to the left. My mom is sitting on the steps and talking to Douglas' wife. My sister and I are playing in the front yard as we see my father drive down the highway and out of site. However, with the roaring of the motorcycle we could hear my dad coming back from where the trees hid him from our site. Down the highway he comes, passing in front of our yard; he was going so fast. He passed my grandparents' house, my Uncle Harry's house, and then there was a curve, and I heard my mom yell out, "O.T."

My mom jumped up faster than I've ever seen her and ran. I ran holding my four year old sisters hand, behind my mom. There he was...my dad...lying in a small canal below the curve of the highway. He had lost control of his motorcycle. My mom painfully recalls seeing his impact as he hit the telephone pole, his white boots going into the air and landing into the canal. I could not go where he was but as I stood there on that curve and edge of the canal, holding my sister so tightly, I couldn't stop crying. I thought and even mumbled quietly, "He's dead" because he laid there so lifeless and still. My mom continued to call out his name over and over and over but he would not respond.

Out of all the houses came other family members to the rescue. We waited for the ambulance to arrive. While waiting I even remember my grandmother coming, walking down to the site. It seemed like forever before the ambulance arrived. Once there, they put my dad in the back and mom started to get in but they said no. One of my adult cousins said, "Yes, she is." Mom got in the front.

I saw the ambulance leave out, hearing the sirens blaring. Mom later said before they were even close to getting to the hospital in Wilmington they had turned off the sirens. He was considered DOA, 'Dead on Arrival'.

At the age of seven, I was fatherless. The precious memories of the motorcycle rides, the late nights in my pajamas riding on dad's tractor when he would come in from his evening shift to go out to the plow and disc fields...there would be no more of that.

So, you see almost a year later, at that moment when I was eight, that was when I heard that Word in my heart it was truly significant. *It was like the beginning of God getting my attention*, yet, not knowing how or what that really meant in my life.

~ I never forgot that moment to this very day ~

# SECTION 2

# Our *Code of Conduct* is the BIBLE

## The Lessons I Learned While Serving In the Military

Chapter 5

The next lesson I learned while in the Military was that you will be challenged.

Not everyone wants you to succeed.

While serving as Dorm Chief there was a particular young airmen who made it undeniably clear that he did not like me. He never said why and to this day I don't know why and I don't lose any sleep over it; it didn't matter. He was going to do all he could to sabotage my responsibilities. When I made assignments and duties he was the first to question them. When I gave him specific tasks he was brazen enough in making it clear that if he did it, it wasn't because I told him to (when in essence it was). His blatant rebellion culminated with him finally challenging me in front of the rest of the trainees.

Now keep in mind, I was designated as the Dorm Chief with all the inherent authority that comes with the title and responsibility; this never should have gotten to this point. I should have addressed him immediately and because I didn't I was confronted with the looming possibility of losing the respect of the trainees.

I discovered something inside of me that rose up and pushed me where I should have been all along.

I gathered the core of me and said, "You want me? Let's do

it!" After sharing a piece of my mind with him, not for show but to put rebellion in its place and secure the respect of the trainees. I then reported him to my Drill Sergeant. When my Drill Sergeant heard about the situation he said, "I will take care of it."

From that day forward I never had another problem with that airman again. I learned something about *authority* and *order*.

With a new inspiration and dedication I worked hard to be the best and to help my Dorm become the best; both my Dorm and I graduated from Basic Training. Transformed from the straggly, indifferent civilians, we had proven ourselves capable of following military standards, dress and ceremony, customs and code of conduct. We were now ready for the next phase of our training; Advance Course.

## **Humble Beginnings**

Chapter 6

<u>It's personal</u>

Now, I am a little girl growing up being raised by a strong single woman. In my opinion she had to be. Yet, it doesn't take the place of having a father, so I had my moments that I cried out and I know God comforted me. My mom kept a tight rope on us to a certain extent but she wanted us to enjoy life as well. Mom's drive came from an inner push wherein she wanted to keep anyone from saying that they had to take care of her girls. For various reasons my mother moved to Riegelwood, NC. It was not too far from her in-laws or her family in East Arcadia; we were about in the middle. She purchased land to raise her girls on. She eventually remarried for a time. At first I gave my stepfather a hard way to go as a pre-teen. At the same time, I couldn't get away with it but so much. All I knew was I yearned for something that even a stepfather could not replace.

I went through different changes. I did not want to fit within the statistics of 'A girl with no father.' I wasn't really happy about being away from my Perkins family (my father's people). Being close to them still gave me parts of him. But eventually it became okay. I wasn't happy about my schools either because I was picked on in elementary and junior high. I was skinny (boney I was called) and felt like an ugly duckling to top it off. Many times I begged my mom to let me go to school somewhere else.

School had started in my local area for 9th grade. I went to school my first day. But after much begging and crying and promising I would do better somewhere else, mom eventually allowed both my sister and me to attend school outside the county in Leland, NC. This was 15 miles from our home, one way but the distance didn't matter to us at all. Often we would see my dad's two sisters, which were married to the two Troy brothers. I was excited. I not only loved my aunties, but I loved myself some Uncle Walter and Uncle Sam too. My Aunt Bernice Perkins (Troy) taught at the middle school where my sister attended. My Aunt Esther Perkins (Troy) taught at the high school where I started and attended as a freshman. It was new beginnings as I excelled academically and socially. I wasn't just a struggling student anymore. Some of the things I accomplished: I was Miss Freshman Queen, student government vice-president, and the sophomore's Miss Homecoming Maid of Honor. I also joined different high school clubs, the high school band, and made all state band contests more than once. I became the high school drum major before graduating. My band director said I was his first pecan tan, (brown skin). It was very good times in my life, and even with that...I still felt there was more for me.

I tried to recall if there was anything specific that was calling me to God but there wasn't; not anything I could remember. My mother said to me that she had noticed that the death of my father did affect me; *I was the one who followed my dad's every footstep.* I always felt my sister was closer to my mom than I was. She had her, and I had no one. However, that was my perception but it wasn't true. Yet, it caused us to have moments of tension when I was a teen. There were also those acts of promiscuity that taunted me, and left me unhappy with feelings of guilt. I need to say this, even one time or a few times is way too many times. I struggled with what I grew up hearing often, "It was up to the guy to ask and the girl to say, no." It wasn't the guys fault but it was my fault for allowing it. I tried to reach out to talk to any of my aunts, not really telling all, but hoping they would understand me or tell me what I really needed to hear.

I'm almost 16 years old now and my stepfather's sister, aunt Deborah (Dixon), who was also married to my mom's first cousin at the time, took me to a prayer meeting with her. I remember being at the prayer meeting, kneeling at the chair for what seemed like hours. The older ladies would be praying and we were told to just call out Jesus' name. They would be over you, saying and calling out, "Jesus, Jesus, Jesus, Jesus" repeatedly and you were to do the same. Calling out in that manner I understood from their understanding was Jesus beginning to save, cleanse, and sanctify you. *I didn't know what I was doing but I did it because I wanted what I felt at eight years old, something that was real.* I am still grateful as I know that these women still loved and wanted God with what they knew.

However, that was not the moment of salvation that was personable to me or real. It wasn't in church, or before a group or crowd of people. I can't tell you what day it was or the exact time like some people can recall. *All I know*...it was one afternoon in my bedroom, alone, the Word God I had heard before came to me, *"That **if you** confess with your mouth the Lord Jesus and **believe in your heart** that God has raised Him from the dead, you will be saved."* I didn't know that was **Romans 10:9** then. *I do know* I was almost 16 years old, and as I sat in my bedroom with its brown panel walls surrounding me, I found myself on my knees, and I made that confession *audibly*. I don't know where anyone else was in the house or even if they were at home, but **that day I accepted Christ truly in my life and it was real**.

It was after that moment that what God had revealed to me at 8 years old and then again when I was almost 16 years old and today at 49 years old – **He is so real, so serene, so personable, so God.**

At 16, we became connected with the Church of God in Christ. This was good for us in certain ways as we connected to young Christian people and it kept my sister and I active. I remember they would sing, "This is the Church of God in Christ, you can't join in...

...you have to be born in, this is the Church of God in Christ." When I look back at it I didn't know *how to be* Church of God in Christ per say. *It was very traditional so I did what others did thinking this would sanctify me and bring me closer to God.* I stopped wearing pants, jewelry etc. If you're from that background you understand. Again, I'm grateful because I know, "Being confident of this very thing, that **He who has begun a good work in me** will perform it until the day of Jesus Christ." **Philippians 1:6**. I also understand today that God will perfect that which pertains to me. **Psalm 138:8**. I know it was in those growing moments my desire for Him was more than what I saw around me and yet, I said very little I just went with the flow.

---

## Me & Tammy, Tammy & Me

Tammy and I are two different people but yet two peas in a pod. Tammy is a free thinking conservative and I'm just conservative, lol. I am not making reference to any political parties either. It's just my best way of explaining the two of us. The two peas in this pod, you can never really separate us.

We're different from my husband's siblings. They love each other dearly but are alright with not communicating on a regular basis. His sisters will rarely call. They usually talk/speak when my husband, their brother does the calling. Tammy and I cannot see each other for days but we communicate at least two and three times a week if not more. When we were young and had our own beds/bedrooms, we would sometimes go in the bedroom with our mom and giggle all night. There were times we would get in trouble and we would get each other in trouble. We fought like any other sisters but we stood up for each other too. The stories we tell today about those times makes us laugh for hours.

The fact that we're so close and yet different is a rarity today. We respect each other's space to a certain extent. There are times we both inconvenience each other for the sake of family, children, or what have you, but it's all good. We call before we step into the others home as we're both married. We know our boundaries when it comes to family, we just have to remind each other sometimes but not often; I say that with a smile.

Once, when my car was parked in Tammy's driveway, a family member thought it was Tammy's because our cars look just alike. The family member asked, ***"When are you two going to stop competing with each other?"*** We both shook our heads to the nonsense knowing just how little they really understood us. I imagine that many of our family think that crazy stuff about us competing but they have no idea. My mom didn't raise us that way. She raised us to have vision in our life and for our lives, and to be there for one another.

We dressed alike when we were little. My mom said she tried one year to break us from it. She took us separately to shop and we still ended up with the same clothes and the same patent leather shoes for church. When one of us had something, we wanted the other to have it too. That hasn't changed much. Turns out, Tammy is more of a shopper and a negotiator than I will ever be. Yet guess what, we still end up with some of the same things in our closet, our home, etc. We get a joy and kick out of it. When buying one we get three. Yes, mom was included and now sometimes Diamond, (my daughter) or Kamora (Tammy's daughter). I look back over the years of the pictures we took together and they highlight so many of the cherished moments in my life.

Tammy does like to be unique, and she is a fly dresser. However, you should see how excited she gets when she puts things together for us. She negotiated the deal for my car, and when she added an extra ornament to her car she wanted me to have it too. She was like, yes come on, we'll be twins.

I am grateful for my family and especially that mom raised us together. Throughout trying times in my life, I didn't always have to give Tammy details but if I had a need she was there trying to make it happen. When she needs me I am the same way. She said something to me one time when working with a young lady. She said mom must have raised us differently. When we knew that one needed something, we'd do our best to make it happen if we could. Yet, Tammy said she watched that young lady in need and not one of her family members, who knew her need, offered to help her.

I'm so grateful we have each other and we wouldn't have it any other way.

To prove my point:

Tammy & Me

↑ Me & Tammy / Me. Mom & Tammy ↓

Mom & Me

My sister – Tammy

Tammy, Mom & Me

# SECTION 3

# Our *DUTY* <u>is</u> to LIVE for JESUS

---

## The Lessons I Learned While Serving In the Military

Chapter 7

Advance Course Training involves the study of your specific AFSC[4] or specialty. I was assigned to Lowry AFB, located in the cities of Aurora and Denver, Colorado to study electronics. God had begun to breakdown my old useless ways of looking at life and it was at Lowry AFB, I had the greatest epiphany that would change my life forever. Having completed Basic Training and now attending advance training, *the reality of my old life and new life suddenly came together.*

*Where was I and where was I going?*

The military had a clear idea of where I was going but I now was faced with the reality that I was here. The question began to resurface...

*...Why are you here?*

---

[4] AFSC – The Air Force Specialty Code (AFSC) is an alphanumeric code used by the United States Air Force to identify an Air Force Specialty (AFS). Officer AFSC's consist of four characters and enlisted AFSC's consist of five characters. A letter prefix or suffix may be used with an AFSC when more specific identification of position requirements and individual qualifications is necessary. The AFSC is similar to the Military Occupational Specialty (MOS) used by the United States Army and the United States Marine Corps or enlisted ratings and USN officer designators and USCG officer specialties used by the United States Navy and the United States Coast Guard.

The answer: Because you made a mess out of your life. The question...

*...Why did you make a mess of your life?*

The answer: Because you did not have any real substance.

Now came the most important question I could ask myself while sitting in my tiny dorm room in the freezing temperatures of Denver, Colorado.

**Where is God in all of this?**

**Is God even real?**

At that moment I said to myself but knew I was really talking to Him...

*"God, if you are real show yourself real to me? If not, I am going to live this life the best way I know how with you or without you."*

Just like that day when the Drill Sergeant first showed up at the platform and got in my face with intensity and presence, I heard in my spirit God say to me...

**"You never made me Lord of your life. You wanted my salvation, but you did not accept my Lordship."**

It shook me when I heard that. He was right, I did not want to go to hell, but I did not live my life the way God wanted me to in His Word. *That moment I made a commitment to give God Lordship of my life.*

That moment my life changed forever.

## **Humble Beginnings**

## Chapter 8

<u>Wanting More…</u>

I was hungry for spiritual depth not outwardly religious norms or religious verbiage/talk around me. It had to be personable, *it had to be real*. I still wrestle with being around 'churchie' (my term) people. Every word out of their mouths is praise the Lord, thank you Jesus, and you can't relate to them because they are of no *earthly* good. And then you have those that talk so deep in conversation and no one is getting any joy out of said conversation but them. I tend to be quiet sometimes around these types.

Then there was another *wanting* in my life.

I wanted a marriage that was different than anything I had seen. It doesn't mean that I did not have good marriages around me but I wanted different/more. My father married my mother but he had many children out of wedlock before and during their marriage. There was a time I would often feel cheated that I didn't have my other siblings there to grow up with me especially the older ones. Some of us are close and some of us are not and some of us don't even really know each other; my brother Craig (Radford) keeps us connected.

I loved my father so much. He left me great memories that I can speak of. He was the dad who let me stand on his feet while I danced with him. He was the dad that would cook me scrambled eggs with hot sauce when I wanted them. He was an awesome dad in my mind but even at six and seven years old I knew he wasn't a good husband to my mom. He was a good friend to many, and his nieces and nephews loved him just like I did. Again, he left behind some good memories and my mom loved him. Yet, he cheated on my mom and often would not be home when she needed him. He actually wounded her by shooting her in her arm with a .38 caliber, claiming he believed she was a burglar. My mom reveals a different story which I believe because I was standing there by the window when it happened. He was still angry because earlier in the day he was made aware of some money he felt my mom hid from him. I was there when he threatened her with the gun but my mom lifted me up in front of her and he stopped coming toward her. My mom endured much and *if you want to know where I get some of my strength, it was from her.*

I also grew up seeing households where men and women were married in name only although they lived together. They were housemates sharing different rooms in the house for years. I wanted more for me; I wanted a man of God, a friend, a lover. I did see some good examples too; there were my neighbors in Riegelwood, NC. No relations to them but my sister and I called them aunt Bee and uncle Bud, they were Mr. and Mrs. James Merritt. I loved that I had the opportunity to see them grow old together and see that they loved each other.

But even more there were the very Christian pillars of my family, my dad's parents. They are a cherished gift in my life. As I recall my grandfather and grandmother, George Douglas Perkins and Sallie Mae Cables Perkins, they were my true good examples. We all call them Big Mama and Big Daddy. Being in their home was experiencing two people growing old together and loving each other. My dad was the baby out of many, and dad had nephews and nieces older than him. My grandparents were in their early 70's when we were children. I know they had been through a lot of things together, and many things we don't know about I am sure. As one of their grandchildren, I watched them and knew they were serious about their walk with God. It was more than my grandfather founding a church building. My grandfather knew his bible like it was the back of his hand. Yet, I never felt like he was preaching at us but showing us how to walk out God's love.

As a teenager/young adult, I remember asking him one day when he and Big mama were sitting in their rocking chairs side by side,

"Big Daddy, do you still love Big Mama the way you did when you were first married?" Big Daddy said, while at the same time reaching over to touch and rub Big Mama's knee, in his grandpa voice, "Yep, Yep, I love her more today than I did yesterday." Yes, that is what I wanted. My grandma was the same way; she was funny and made us laugh. She would talk about subjects that you would not normally feel comfortable talking about with your grandmother or with a Christian person for that matter. I believe she made all of her grandchildren feel like they had a special part in her life. She would say the craziest things to us and give you her best wisdom on subjects such as sex and being wife. Even my mom says that today, "Big Mama was a woman of wisdom." She talked about saving yourself for marriage and in the same breath talked about what to do if you feel like you were burning to keep you from falling. It was hilarious. They both were 95 years old when they passed away, my grandfather leaving first and my grandmother three years later.

Big Mama & Big Daddy holding hands still as I remember

## The Lessons I Learned While Serving In the Military

Chapter 9

When I began my advance studies, I experienced God's presence and help in everything I did. I started going to Chapel every Sunday, actually every opportunity I had. I yearned for understanding in life and living which led me to study the Bible for needed direction. By this time my estranged wife made it clear she no longer considered our marriage a marriage and she wanted an annulment. That relationship dissolved but I determined not to go down with it. So, I made a commitment to not look for another relationship but to *seek God first.*

I began to see myself succeed like I never had succeeded before. I was placed in a leadership position in my class; I did exceedingly well in my studies. I fought off temptations to do evil as Jesus admonished us to pray, **"And don't let us yield to temptation, but rescue us from the evil one." (Matthew 6:13)** By the time I graduated from my advance course I had developed a deeper walk with God and belief in myself. Graduating with honors, I requested to go anywhere in the world, something you did not do in the military. I was assigned Patrick AFB, Brevard County, Florida. My first assignment was on the beach.

Flying from Denver, Colorado to Melbourne, Florida was like abruptly going from night to day. The brand new person I had become was now going to be tested immediately upon landing in Florida. When I arrived, I was picked up by my

NCO[5] and members of my unit.

"Get in Airman Busch; we're going to welcome you to sunny Florida."

"Great…" was my reply. "…where are we going?"

"We're going to take you to the hottest strip club in Cocoa Beach and get you familiar with your new assignment." My NCO said excitedly. Instantly my alarms went off.

What am I going to do!?! Going to a strip club was definitely not what God wanted me to do, but this is my boss and co-workers. What are they going to think if I tell them I can't go?

In that instant I heard myself say, "Take me home, I cannot go to the strip club, I am a Christian."

I could hear a feather drop in that car. With a shrug and evident disappointment my new NCO turned the car around and took me to my new barracks. I sure made a great impression with my new unit; I was the 'Holy Roller.'

---
[5] NCO – Non Commissioned Officer

## Humble Beginnings

Chapter 10

<u>Getting more</u>

I shared all of these things about my past so you can relate more closely to my past, present, and my future with H. James Busch, Jr.

I was in college now, and I was dating a young minister I had started dating my junior/senior year of high school. We had some rocky times trying to walk out our salvation and be in a relationship with each other. We were in a growing, thriving church and closely connected together with our leader, Pastor Otis Locket, who we both saw as our spiritual father. As the church grew, I think I took it personally, as I felt our pastor was more concerned with him than me, a young lady. It was the men he was compelled to minister to I felt, and rightfully so. But again, it was my perception.

One thing I am so grateful for is that he made me really learn and memorize scriptures. Although there were several significant scriptures, there was one of great importance to me which I will share later. Despite having such a wonderful church and pastor, I felt a lot of deep hurt there and I wasn't proud of how I responded. I just left. I did my escape and participated with co-op training with the government, NASA in Florida. After my first semester of co-op, I came back to school in Greensboro, NC, only to leave again. After finishing my 2$^{nd}$ semester of co-op term I decided not to go back to NC A&T State University again. I transferred my records and I really left this time.

I was attending a Church of God in Christ church in Cocoa, Florida. My pastor there treated me like a daughter. I called him Daddy Taylor, who was in his late 70's or early 80's I believe. I had met a young man while working at NASA on my third semester. We were dating and this young man showed much interest in me. However, Daddy Taylor did not want me dating anymore he said. I listened and broke up with my engineer boyfriend who was working for Lockheed *then*. That young man went to talk to Daddy Taylor and changed his mind. He said, "That young man really likes you." So, my pastor gave me his blessings. Yet, during that time we were missing something together. He had given me a promise ring and eventually wanted me to marry him. He was also a home body and I wanted to do more things of interest to me. However, his focus was saving for his mom's house etcetera, and I truly respected that. Yet, I wasn't the type you had to spend a lot of money on but he didn't quite get that. I remember sharing with my mother and Tammy (my sister) on their previous visit what I felt like I was missing from this 'so nice' relationship. I said to mom, "Even going to the beach doesn't cost you anything." She said to me then, "If it hasn't changed now what makes you think it will change when you get married?" I pondered that question. Before I left to study abroad in Europe I was going to give the young man back his ring; however, my plan was to think about it more on the trip. Upon my return, I gave him back the ring. I had made up my mind that I wasn't looking for a relationship or anything else.

*I made up my mind to focus on serving God.* During that same time, Daddy Taylor wanted me to prepare to minister more. I started studying and preparing for this in my life.

Also during this time, my young sister, who was in high school, was coming to spend the summer with me. I moved out of my one bedroom apartment to a two bedroom apartment just to accommodate her coming. She was excited about this as she got to stay the summer with her sister and work a job before her senior year in high school. On one of her previous visits, she met a young Air Force airman at the church I was attending. They continued to communicate when she went back to her college prep boarding school. But now the summer was here and so was she.

# SECTION 4

# Our *Military Operation* is the KINGDOM of GOD

## The Lessons I Learned While Serving In the Military

### Chapter 11

When I completed 'In Processing' and was placed in my assignment I was given the detail to clean up the parts area. Of course this area was a total mess and was given to the lowest person in rank as initiation to their new assignment and a reminder of their inferior status.

What I learned next taught me the *power of following God's Word*.

In the Bible it says when someone asks you to go a mile, instead go two. In the military you are taught to only do what you are assigned and never do more than you are asked.

I decided to follow God.

So, I took my new assignment as the parts organizer and spent my off duty time working on organizing and labeling the parts so that it would be the most organized parts section in the unit. After working several days on this assignment, I finished the project in such a way that the Civilian Chief of the Department said this was the best parts section he had ever seen and from that moment on I was given favor.

God's way. **Proverbs 3:1 & 4, *"Never forget the things I have taught you. Store my commands in your heart. Then you will find favor with God and people, and you will earn a good reputation."***

When I was assigned to the production studio I discovered the hidden cache of X-rated videos that should not have been there and I erased *every one* of them. When extra volunteer positions where requested, I volunteered.

Over time the godly standard I had taken instead of being ridiculed was beginning to be respected. What's even more shocking is the rowdiest and wildest person in our unit was a backslidden Christian. Because of my stand for God, he started going back to church and *rededicated his life to Christ*.

God gave me so much favor that I was called on to minister to my non-commissioned officer's (NCO's) when they were going through marriage problems.

Because of the standard I had established I began to excel in my work and I was selected below the Zone Sergeant, and step promoted to Staff Sergeant. In two years I went from being an Airman to a Staff Sergeant.

Of course, all success must come with challenges. In this case the challenge came to me from a higher ranking Staff Sergeant who felt it was his responsibility to bring me back to earth. So, shortly thereafter he began to question what I was doing and why I was doing it. When I was given an assignment to participate in an honor guard detail for which I was an honor guard the sergeant decided to write me up for not being available for duty. I reported his statement to the head non-commissioned officer and the sergeant was reassigned to another section.

Again, *God showed me favor*.

*I contribute all of my success to God showing Himself real to me because of my commitment to make Jesus Lord of my life.* I was chosen Airman of the year for my base and nominated for Airman of the Year for the entire Air Force.

This was quite a change for a man who had made a mess of his life.

I was called in by the Base Commander and told that he would recommend me for Officers Candidate School (OCS) and to let him know what position I was interested in. I told him I wanted to be a Chaplain. I could see the disappointment in his face as he said he could not help me with that, but for me, my commitment to God was my life and purpose.

*If I was going to be in the military, I wanted to do it for God.*

# NEWS

*8 The Missileer December 6, 1985*

SrA. Howard J. Busch Jr. — USAF photo by Ursula Spitzer

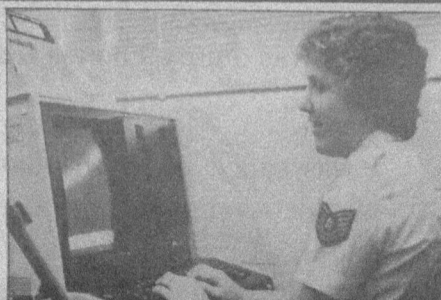
TSgt. Donna Painter — USAF photo by TSgt. Earl Catchings

## Two earn stripes for exceptional performance

**From staff reports**

Two Patrick members, TSgt. Donna Painter and SrA. Howard J. Busch Jr., received promotions through the Stripes for Exceptional Performers (STEP) Program during November.

Sergeant Painter, the NCOIC of administration at the Air Force Technical Applications Center, received her promotion Nov. 25 and was immediately eligible to pin on her stripe. Sergeant Painter received the promotion because of her overall outstanding duty knowledge and performance in addition to her extensive involvement in community activities and AFTAC sports.

Airman Busch, a television specialist with the 2179th Communications Group, will pin on staff-sergeant stripes May 2 of next year. Airman Busch is a graduate of the University of California, Davis campus.

A recent recipient of the Air Force Achievement Medal, Airman Busch is a member of the Patrick Honor Guard and involved in community activities.

## **Humble Beginnings**

### Chapter 12

<u>Eighteen days that changed my life</u>

It was going to be my sister Tammy's birthday soon. So, I asked some of my friends at the church including Mark, (the Air Force airman that Tammy was friends with), to bring some of the young men he always brought with him to church to Pizza Hut so we can celebrate my sister's birthday. It was normal for Mark to bring young men to church with him, but none of them ever got my attention.

However, little did I know on the mind of one of those young men, was me. He later told me, "I saw you sitting on the front pew."

It's now the evening of June 11, 1985, we were at Pizza Hut for Tammy's birthday celebration. My engineer, career-driven ex-boyfriend even came. Mark was there and he had brought another young man with him. Soon after he settled in he told me he also invited his friend, James who *may* be joining us. We had ordered our pizzas and were sitting and talking, then who walks in the door – James Busch. I figured this could be him since Mark told me he was probably coming. I also vaguely remember he may have been one the guys I saw sitting in the back of the church with Mark before. I got up from the long table and went to introduce myself. He introduced himself as James. I said thanks for coming. I also mentioned we had already ordered pizzas and suggested he order something before he came to the table; something along those lines.

But it was everything after this introduction that became purposeful.

He said to me, "You know I had the option to go play basketball or come here, but I chose to come here." He was letting me know then that he had a purpose for coming. However, I didn't get it that clearly then, I thought he was just talking. He sat on one end of the table where most of the guys were and I, my sister, and the other young ladies from the church were at the other end of the table. As a matter of fact, I believe he and my ex-boyfriend were sitting right next to each other. My friend Tina started saying how cute James was and wanted to draw my attention to him. Then my sister chimes in on the conversation and tells me she is inviting him over after the dinner. I don't remember all of what happened after that other than he was planning to come over to our place. However, after the party, my ex-engineer friend was having trouble with his car and asked me to follow him home. It took an hour to go and come back as he lived in Melbourne, FL about 30 minutes away from Cocoa, FL where I lived.

After I returned, James was there in my apartment. We talked for a little bit, and somehow we got on the subject of a message I was preparing on Psalm 23. Not very long after that, it was getting close to 10:00 pm, James told me he needed to leave because he had a curfew for himself. What??? I was impressed that a young man had enough discipline to put himself on a curfew. I liked that, besides I had to go to work myself the next day at NASA. I was still working there as an engineering student. That was June 11, 1985, a Tuesday, the day I meet Howard James Busch Jr., whom I called, James.

Wednesday, June 12th seemed like just another day at work and home. Tammy started working her job at McDonalds down the street also. In the late afternoon she and Mark would be out sometimes so I was home alone.

Then...my phone rings and the male voice on the other side says, "Hi, this is James. I hope you don't mind, but I got your number from Mark." I was thinking laughingly how dare Mark give my number out without asking me? Then he went on further to say, "I am attracted to you, and I feel the feeling is mutual; however, if not, let me know, I will not waste your time or mine" he says calmly. I can feel and remember that caught off guard surprised look on my face, as if to say in my mind, this is really bold, but I like it. So, I replied with a slight hesitancy but truthfulness, "Yes, I'm attracted to you but..." He interrupts, and says something along these lines, "Mark told me that you just had a breakup so I understand you want to take your time." In my mind, I am thinking again, "I'm going to get Mark for telling my business, (laughing inside)." But again I replied, "Yes, I don't want to rush getting into any relationships right now." My focus was on getting myself together and preparing to minister on that coming Friday. I don't think we talked long but we made a date to see each other the next evening. I called my mom, and told her about him and what he said. She said to me, "Whatever you do, just pray about it and take your time."

It's now Thursday, and James comes over after work. He tells me we are going for a ride to the boardwalk near the beach. He continues to tell me he wants to tell me about himself, and boy did he tell me about himself! He laid it on me all in one night I think. He shared his childhood, his joy, his pain, his divorce, his love and loss of his grandfather, his tears. Without reservation he became transparent and vulnerable before me, a young lady whom he had only known less than two days. I found myself crying with him as I saw both strength and weakness. I saw a man. We continued to enjoy the evening on the boardwalk. It wasn't raining but the night was overlaid with the beautiful moonlit sky. A scene James said he likes seeing over the water.

It's Friday, and it's also my night to speak at the church. James is there as well as my ex because he also knew that I was preparing to speak. It was a bit awkward but not something I gave a lot of attention to as I was prepared to deliver the message God had given me. I did not tell Daddy Taylor (my pastor) about James. He saw him there and the ex. Daddy Taylor had strong opinions about any young man showing interest in me, so I kept that one to myself. The next few days so many things happen but this is what I remember and I will share in the best way I can the order just not the exact days.

James comes over afterwards that Friday, and he was there in my apartment approximately less than 30 minutes I believe. It was getting close to his curfew time again; the impressive and disciplined man he was. He stands at my door to leave, and he asks to hug me before he leaves. So he hugs me and he says, like he almost stuttering, "Andrea, I like, I like, I like, no, I love you. I know you can't say that right now but you will." My response was a sweet silence and I smiled at him. He left out. I thought to myself that was deep, bold, yet sweet, but no, I wasn't going to say that until I knew it.

# SECTION 5

## Our *Soldiering Skills* are to FIGHT the GOOD FIGHT of FAITH

## The Lessons I Learned While Serving in the Military

### Chapter 13

In June 1985, I met a beautiful fired up Christian woman and after knowing her for only eighteen days, (this is not an error. Yes, in only 18 days), we got married. It would've been sooner but it took me that long to convince her; I wanted to marry her the very first day I met her! Andrea Nevoria Perkins became my wife, (we've been married for over 29 years).

With the approval of an early out, I left the Air Force to attend Seminary so I could become a Chaplain in the Military. After leaving active duty I was given a direct commission to the Chaplain Candidate program. While completing my Seminary training I completed assignments at Fort Riley, KS; Fitzsimmons Army Medical Center (AMC) in Aurora, CO; Fort Leavenworth, KS; Fort Leonard Wood, MO and Fort Jackson, SC. In 1990 I graduated from Oral Roberts with a master's degree with honors. Despite being at a great church and recommended for a reserve Chaplain position with a unit in Tulsa, highlighted by my wife delivering our newborn son Joshua; I made critical mistakes in judgment. Simply put, I missed my direction because I didn't listen to the voice of God and allowed *my fears of the style of ministry I was learning* to overwhelm me. So instead, after graduation I chose to move to North Carolina with my wife and brand new baby boy.

Now in North Carolina I awaited my selection back into

active duty. I applied for the Chaplaincy and was denied. The Military was going through a drawdown (a reduction of personnel) during that time and I was not selected back for active duty immediately. In earnestness, I attempted to start a full time ministry but after experiencing frustration, disappointment, and a lack of financial income these realities had me struggling for answers. I left my family in North Carolina to look for work in Ohio, then Denver, Colorado.

I did not realize at the time this was another wilderness period.

I faced many *severe* personal and marital challenges. After experiencing my own semblance of crucifixion, death and resurrection the Lord called me to the Chaplaincy at Fort Braggs, NC. My first assignment was with the 37th Air Borne Engineer Battalion. I served as Chaplain at Smoke Bomb Hill Chapel for the Protestant congregation. I was then placed as Chaplain for the Gospel Service in the 82nd Division.

During an airborne night operation with my unit, *I suffered a head injury that would both enhance and disable my life and ministry...*

I jumped with full cognizance and vigor but when I awakened my first thought was, I made it...I'm in Heaven. Only to realize when a nurse arrived I was in a hospital.

In describing the impact of my head injury, I use the word enhance because I came into a heightened spiritual awareness after my injury. I say disabled because I also became explosive and passionate to the point where I sometimes put myself in potentially precarious situations that could have resulted in serious discipline. Despite it all, God used me during this critical time.

I was later assigned to the 21st Infantry Battalion in Hawaii to serve as Chaplain. I was also selected to be the head Pastor of the Schofield Barracks Gospel Service, a position usually selected for LTC[6] or above.

God showed me favor once again.

My time and service as the 21st Infantry Chaplain and Schofield Barracks Chaplain was phenomenal as God moved in powerful ways throughout both assignments. It wasn't until the intensity of serving in both capacities escalated that the unidentified residuals of my head injury began to take a toll. Finally after experiencing bouts of depression, moments of impulsive behavior, and extreme fatigue I went to a medical doctor who specialized in Traumatic Brain Injury (TBI). They let me know all that was occurring was a direct result of the injury I experienced from the airborne jump.

[6] LTC – Lieutenant Colonel

## **Humble Beginnings**

Chapter 14

<u>Still in the Eighteen life changing days</u>

The next thing I remember is James inviting me to come to Patrick, Air Force Base, to watch him play in a basketball game. After the game he invited me to his dorm room in the barracks. When we arrived, I noted how he left his door completely open. He told me he didn't want anyone to get the wrong impression with a young lady in his room and he wanted to protect me as well. He said *he didn't want our good to be spoken evil of.* I found myself just loving this conviction about him so much.

Somehow we got on the discussion of marriage.

So he wanted to show me these letters he had written over and over again to me. There were several papers all balled up in the trash can basket. He took them out for me and unfolded them. I began to read them and in each of them he was trying to express that he knew it had only been a short time but he wanted to marry me. My mind was thinking is this really happening? We talked more about his letters and how he really wanted to tell me that he does want to marry me. So, before I knew it I heard my mouth saying, "Sure, but you have to ask my parents." (In this case, my mom and stepfather at the time.) That was like a test to me. In the past when I told a young man he had to ask my parents to date me if they weren't serious they wouldn't ask. But James says immediately, "Okay, give me the number." So, I did.

I still hadn't told James I loved him that I recalled. However, I do remember as I was going through this unparalleled courtship, I was in my apartment, my bedroom, praying and crying out to the Lord. I remember some time back asking my pastor's wife in Greensboro, Barbara Locket, how she knew she loved Pastor Otis Locket and she shared as though God had just placed that love for him there in her heart and she knew it. I told God I didn't want to say I love you to anyone again unless it was going to be the real thing. That night I prayed and cried myself to sleep. That next morning the love I had for James had awakened within me; it was there in my heart. I knew now I could tell him that I love him. One of the following evenings when he was leaving for home, I told him that I loved him, and he was so happy!

## Back to the marriage proposal

The very next time I see James, he tells me, "I called your parents." I was shocked! He proceeds to tell me about the conversation with my mom and my stepfather, Freddie Brown. That's a funny story by itself. He said my mom was like, "This is my baby, etc... ", but my stepfather is very short and to the point. He says, "Yes, but if you feel like you gonna beat her..." he says, "...send her home." Little did he know the character of my family, especially my stepfather, but he thought it was funny.

On one of our dates during the 18 days, he also wanted to take me to his job and show me where he worked. It may have been the same night he asked me to marry him, and I went to his basketball game. We went to his job and he showed me around. At some point he reached over to kiss me. It was but a peck on the lips but it was electrifying for us both. After that he said to me, "We will never kiss again until we are married." Whew, he was making sure I knew he was not going to ask me to do anything that would compromise us as Christians. It was right then that I rewrote the old phrase, 'It is up to the guy to ask and the girl to say no.' The new phrase was and I promised myself I would teach my children, *'It is up to the guy to never ask, and the girl doesn't have to say, no.'*

Remember now, it's still June and I believe it had been almost two weeks. He told his parents who lived in Sacramento, California about me, our marriage plans etc. We had been talking about August of the following year or current year I believe. However, one day when riding in the car he looked over to me and said I don't want to wait until August. I think I said, "Me neither." Next thing I know I was calling my mom and telling her we were going to get married that coming Saturday, June 29, 1985. While telling her about it, and she asked concerned, "Why so soon?", but I said *"Mom, He is the one."* I could tell she was struggling with it. But on June 28th, James, Tammy and I drove to the South of the Border, Dillon, SC. While on our way there we took turns driving from Florida but this time I was driving and James was asleep in the passenger's seat. Tammy, my sister, was also sleeping but woke up crying from a dream. I asked her what was wrong. She said to me, "I had a dream about you and James." She said, "He is the one. Nobody knows like I do the hurt you have felt and what you have been through." (Referring to the high school/college boyfriend back in Greensboro, NC.) She said, *"James is the one. He really loves you."*

We arrived in Dillon, SC having a good time that night before our big day. Tammy and I shared a room and James was in the room next door. The next morning I was getting dressed and my mom and stepfather had arrived. My mom and stepfather met James first, and mom came into our room. *Mom seemed excited for the first time.* She bought me this big bag of wedding goodies. I said to her, "Mom, you sound so much better about this." She told me she had been praying all week since I had called. *From her prayers, the Lord told her to release me.* That she did, we went to the marriage chapel to be married. My aunties from NC also drove there to see us get married. **So in eighteen days I married my husband James Busch on June 29, 1985**, and two months later August 31st, we had a reaffirmation church wedding before family and friends in Bolton, NC. It was on the day of my reaffirmation wedding that my grandfather who could not attend the wedding sent for James and I to come to him. People were still at the reception but we went to my grandfather, and he laid his hands on both my husband and I, prayed over us and blessed our marriage; even as the Scriptures have shown us.

It is the foundation of those eighteen days that brought us together as husband and wife and keeps us together *believing for greatness in our marriage and with one another* regardless of any past challenges we've had.

**1985**

1990 Graduation from ORU and birth of JOSHUA

1998

1998

1995

2003

2005

2008

# SECTION 6

# Our *Sacrifice* is to DIE to SELF and LIVE for GOD

## **The Lessons I Learned While Serving in the Military**

### Chapter 15

A harsh reality starred me in the face but I finally realized I could not keep pace with what the Military demanded and just prior to the second Iraq invasion was medically discharged in 1999.

I felt lost. I didn't know what I was going to do and my wife was really concerned for us and our welfare, but I kept telling her to trust God as He would provide.

I started a church this time in Hawaii. I also worked as a High School special education teacher, and a vocational rehabilitation counselor. The pressure and struggles took a major toll on me and I was hospitalized at Tripler Army Medical Center (AMC). After being a patient at Tripler AMC, I was sent to the Veterans Brain Injury Unit in Palo Alto, CA for treatment.

During this time, I found myself in another wilderness period. Yet, God provided for all our needs and sustained us during this extremely difficult time. Right after September 11, 2001, Andrea received an offer to work for the Norfolk Naval Station in Virginia. After living in Virginia Beach for 2 years, she later accepted a position to work for the U.S. Capital Police in Washington, DC.

Things were starting to look up and we moved into our new home in March 2006 in Maryland. It was during this period that our son Joshua began going through a complex change. Joshua became severely ill and this challenged both my wife and I. Looking back Joshua was always the well behaved child in and out of class. He was often a teacher's favorite because he never caused trouble. In addition, Joshua was a very smart student but suddenly he no longer cared about his studies, his sports activities, his instruments. After attempting to get him help at a Military Adolescent Psychology Center, we sought other help. It turns out that they were not able to help or diagnose what was really wrong with our son; as a result he continued to get worse. Refusing to give up or accept their prognosis, we sent Joshua to a wilderness facility in North Carolina that specialized in the treatment of troubled adolescent behavior. What we thought would help Joshua actually made him worse as the facility failed to properly identify his disorder as well. In my son's continual struggle with his unknown illness, on returning home from the wilderness facility Joshua, (not being himself), physically attacked me and I had to press charges *just to get him the help* he desperately needed! I eventually requested the charges be dropped. At that point, a Social Worker recommended us to the Fort Belvoir Adolescent Treatment facility where Joshua was diagnosed with a Mental illness (his brain produced too much dopamine); a disorder that can show up between the ages of 15 and 35 years old. After completing a special program reinforced by the appropriate medication, my son began to settle down. He was enrolled in a special education program at Bowie High School which was provided to him after much effort on our part. Without question, this was the provision of God with the support of one special Individual Education Program teacher.

Joshua's behavior began to regress again. Finally after being admitted into the hospital for over a month, Joshua was transferred to a residential treatment facility in Virginia Beach, VA. The treatment at the Residential Facility was still not going well. We were really beginning to ask God why our son was suffering from this illness. A secondary but major issue was the overall cost to take care of Joshua which had taken its emotional and financial toll on the family. In my wife's attempt to take care of both me and Joshua, Andrea was forced to resign from her position with the Capital Police. We really struggled financially, almost losing our home.

We stood fast believing in God to help us.

After several months of treatment and being denied additional treatment at the Residential Facility, Joshua came home and was provided an excellent female doctor at Walter Reed who got Joshua on the right medication. After much prayer and hard work we were able to get Joshua into a level five education program called High Roads Academy. Once Joshua's illness was diagnosed, the military temporarily assigned a heath care case manager who assisted us through the treatment process. Before having to leave this assignment, she said this to us....*she had never seen parents fight so hard for the life and well-being of their son.*

What we learned through this experience or illness is that many teens and adults often are lost due to non-diagnosis and improper treatment of their mental illness. As a result they end up being criminalized or marginalized in life because they do not receive the proper help or treatment. We refused to let that be Joshua's life. We believed and continue to believed God for our son's abundant life.

To the glory of God, in 2010 Joshua graduated from High

School with his diploma.

Andrea had not worked for quite a while devoting all of her/our attention on helping Joshua. Diamond, our daughter had not been in the same schools for very long due to the number of moves and we wanted to provide her with an opportunity to go through her High School years in the same school. Diamond was accepted into Elizabeth Seton High School; initially we couldn't afford to pay the tuition. We believed God for a miracle and despite having to go through major obstacles with the new president we were able to get her through her freshman year. Eventually, Andrea was hired by a federal contractor, and a year later back with a major federal agency. Diamond graduated from Elizabeth Seton High School in May of 2013.

God never failed to help us in our time of need regardless of any circumstances, bureaucracy or minimizations we faced.

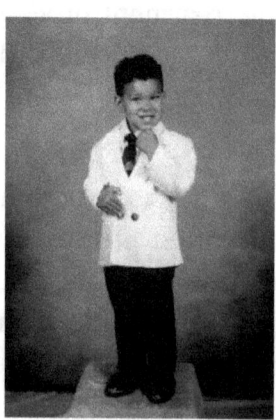

## Humble Beginnings

Chapter 16

<u>What was it like being married to James?</u>

When two people come together in marriage they bring who they are into the marriage.

His past, my past intertwined to then start our lives together to build a future from our then current and present life. James was a city boy from Sacramento, California, me a southern country girl. Although his family had deep roots in the Church of God in Christ denomination in California, James' parents distanced themselves from that and he was raised in the Christian Reformed Church. I was raised in the Southern Baptist and then Pentecostal, Church of God in Christ.

James is a free spirit, a risk taker. Me, in general, I like following all the rules and having structure. It was our melting pot to make something that would taste good yet, the heat of life had to be applied in order to make it good; to get the flavor right. *This applied, ordained heat let us see what was in us and what needed to come out of us.* If I had to bring it all together, I would use this quote I heard from a movie called, 'Return to me.'

**"It's the character that's the strongest that God gives the most challenges to."**

It's amazing to be able to say that today because at a point in my life although I was very independent, I also thought of myself as being somewhat weak. It was in my marriage to James that I learned to SOAR, (which I share and explain later). Maybe the biblical origins of our names meant something together. His first name is Howard which I'm told means *courage,* and James is *truth.* My name Andrea has a meaning of *strong woman.* And even my nickname, Angie means *messenger* or *messenger of God.* Be it true or not, I don't necessarily study the meanings of names and their origins, (someone gave me a name plague as a gift with a scripture).

I grew in my marriage to James in so many ways. Being married to James was and is like a breath of fresh air.

At the very same time there have also been many growing pains that would either break us or make us; this was the heat in our melting pot. Each challenge God would use to grow me up in Him. Each victory and celebration was a building of faith, a demonstration of God's love and grace for the next level or purpose he had for us in our walk together with our heavenly Father.

We challenged each other in the way we grew up, especially him. It wasn't meant to be in a negative way, but James would ask the challenging questions of what was really tradition, bondage, or true freedom in Christ and mostly what was biblical. Not that tradition was all bad either, but his quest made me think and really seek after God's heart. Having come out of Church of God in Christ at the time, I didn't wear make-up, but he wanted me to feel free to do so. James was always saying to me that I had a natural beauty with or without make up but it wasn't the make-up that was the focus, it was my relationship with God. He likewise was challenged to grow into living out what it meant to be led by the Spirit, to have faith. We both eventually within our first year of marriage joined a charismatic Bible teaching church to grow together.

I grew up with strong work ethics, but he showed me something more than just working hard; always giving your best when working. James was a demonstration of this when

I met him as he carried out his duties as an airman. I was there when he made it to his below the zone promotions. When I reflect back over the past years of my career, every evaluation I had as an officer in the Army Reserves or as a civilian in the government work place demonstrated what I learned from seeing my husband daily, a man of excellence.

Also of great importance, what I learned from my husband is even in the struggles we had to work through **never sacrificing family**. Although there were times where we both failed at this, and I will share more later, we both have come back to it over and over again of a true meaning of what that is. We were living on Patrick Air Force Base in the beginning of our marriage. The first year, I was still working for NASA Kennedy Space Center as a co-op engineer student. On the day James was to be honored as Airman of the Year and I was leaving work, the car breaks down on that long strip coming out of NASA to the gate. Along the sides of that two lane highway, it was not unusual to see alligators on the side of the highway. Mobile phones were not in your cars as a norm. This meant me walking to the gate. I kept hoping a car would come along but I did not see any and time was ticking. I was afraid to walk to the gate but I had to let James know what happened. I made it to the gate and called James. He told me he would get Mark, his friend, and come and get me. But I told him if he did that he wouldn't make it to the banquet on time. He said to me, "You are more important." I was concerned because this was not only finding out if he made the "Airman of the Year" but there was a gentlemen from Washington, DC who was going to be at that banquet whom we were told was on the board that makes a determination for James' below the zone[7] promotion. James was also on the color guard and this

---

[7] Below the Zone - (BZ) or secondary zone promotion capability is designed to allow the accelerated promotion of outstanding officers who have demonstrated performance and indicated potential clearly superior to those who otherwise would be promoted.

meant they were expecting him there at the beginning for the rifle and flag presentation. He showed me then that family was important to him. He came out to meet me with Mark. We left the car and rushed back to our home. Both Mark and I helped him get into his color guard dress uniform. We rushed to the banquet. Everyone was in place and the color guard was just getting ready to march in. James' commander could see that he was late and had joined in just in time. That night when we were sitting down after the dinner, his commander came over and asked James why he was late. He said sir, "My wife's car broke down and I had to go get her." The commander said to him, "Good choice son, good choice." I was relieved in a way, but we still waited to hear about the below zone selection. The good news is he did receive that below the zone promotion with his honor and priorities in place.

# SECTION 7

# Our *Mission* is to MAKE DISCIPLES

---

## **The Lessons I Learned While Serving in the Military**

A Closing Thought – **D.R.I.V.E.**

**"Whether I live or die, blessed be the name of the Lord"**

Even I was writing the enemy tried to delete these last words; all I did was hit, "REDO."

I'm retired from the military but I'm now full in spirit and refueled for the mission. I am determined to D.R.I.V.E. on.

What drives me and what hides me? I really wanted to become a great person. I wanted to be either a great athlete or a powerful, charismatic leader. When I struggled to communicate, and when I discovered I couldn't run fast or jump high I kept on trying. I believed, if I kept trying hard enough maybe one day the great leader or athlete switch would turn on and I would realize my dream.

### **DETERMINATION**

In elementary school I experienced an embarrassing situation while trying to tell a joke. I felt ridiculed by another student, and it resulted in an inner fear to express myself. These issues grew, becoming bigger fears during my growing years, and as an adult. They affected my confidence to communicate effectively and my ability to perform. Despite these feelings I did have one thing that helped me to overcome my fears and that was *a faith in God's help and a willingness to step out!*

When my mother first enrolled me in swimming lessons, I felt like I could swim after the first class. When the class was over I walked over to the deep water, (10 feet), and jumped in expecting to swim. To my surprise the strokes they showed me were not holding me above the water and I began to sink. Just as unexpected as the possibility that I might drown, was the hand from underneath the water that lifted me out of the pool. *I realize now, the Lord was watching over me.*

On my first day of High School during PE class we gathered together to play football. When deciding positions I boldly stated, "Let me be the quarterback." After several hikes it became apparent that I neither had the speed nor arm to be a quarterback and I was fired from my position; someone more capable took over. I went from feeling large to feeling small. There was some incongruence in my thinking and my performance that began to cause me to withdraw.

Another day in PE the teacher decided to have the slowest runners race against each other. Qualifying for that designation I was placed as the anchor. Despite my team having an early lead in the relay handoff, I still lost to a very overweight student only confirming that I could not run with speed. You can imagine how humiliating that was.

Still determined to discover my gift; I decided that if I could not run fast, maybe I could run long. So, I tried out for the cross country track team. Despite never having run seriously I decided to run a twelve mile course. To say the least, I came in last, elevating the overall cross country team points (opposite of good) and my cross country running career came to a skittering halt.

I then attempted to try out for the football team. Weighing only 99 lbs, having no speed, or real muscles, but fearless, I attempted to run and block the more athletically gifted students. It should have come as no surprise I was the first to be cut from the roster.

Well what about basketball? I spent countless hours playing basketball in my front yard and I believed if I kept practicing one day I might even jump and dunk like Dr. J. So, why not try out for the High School basketball team? Again, to my chagrin I was the first to be cut from the team during tryouts.

I took this determination and translated it into outdoor adventures. I had a friend equally as risk-taking and determined as me and together we experienced some great adventures that could have led to death if it had not been for God. Take for example our fishing trip into the California Sierra Mountains without a map or directions. We took off for a lake. Discovering it had been frozen over and we couldn't fish there we figured, if we went even deeper we could find another lake. So off we went, and we did find another lake; broke out the fishing rods and had a great fishing experience. Now came the problem, we didn't know where we were. So, looking at the setting sun we figured the roads must be over the mountain so off we walked. After several hours we finally found a road and made it back to the car we came in. Looking back, we discovered we traveled on a most challenging course that even professional trail hikers would require the use of sophisticated compasses and maps. We were simply young, foolish, and given mercy!

I can remember another high adventure where I went on a 500 mile bike ride from Sacramento California to Mount Shasta. With only a Sears 10-speed bike I rode with other young men who had expensive racing bikes. I completed the entire ride despite getting shot at by someone in a passing truck, hearing the bullet whizz pass my ear.

Speaking about near death experiences, one of the most subtle yet potentially life ending experiences was one where we were preparing to go to a church basketball game; I found what looked like a toy gun in the brush against the church. I picked up the gun and asked the person next to me if he thought the gun was real. Taking it from my hand he placed it against my head and said, "Let's find out." He playfully pulled the trigger back and at that instant I pushed his hands away and said, "Don't put that thing against my head." Laughing he turned the gun around and pointed it toward a field and pulled the trigger. Bang! The gun went off. We were stunned beyond belief. The gun was real! The police were called and it turned out that the weapon had been used in a robbery of the 7-11 store across the street. That was again another moment my life flashed before my eyes.

## Revelation

Going into the military was an excellent fit for me. It helped me to overcome my lack of athleticism by insisting I meet military standards and fulfillment of the motto, **"Be all you can be."** With that, the opportunity to jump out of helicopters and airplanes was a natural high for me. While serving as a Chaplain for the 37$^{th}$ Airborne Combat Engineers it was nothing for me to be where the soldiers would do live fire, and explosives. Not just on the outside looking in, but in the area of action. One particular day the Engineers were placing an explosive device for demolition of a barrier, (Concertina razor wire). The explosive device was laid and initiation triggered. Leaving the area one of the soldiers BDU's[8] was snagged by the razor wire. Yelling out his dilemma, we immediately went back to free the soldier before the device exploded. After several pulls and tugs I recognized our lives were in immediate danger, so asking for a knife we cut the soldiers pants and with fury proceeded to leave the blast area clearing just seconds before the explosion. This was the everyday life of a Combat Engineer. I really give honor and glory to God for protecting me despite my tendency to get into dangerous situations.

Once while on Chaplain Duty I received a call from a man who said he had a shotgun and was going to kill himself. Immediately I went into intervention mode and asked him why and to stay on the line with me until we could figure this out. What was amazing about this incident is that this individual wasn't even in the military. How could a civilian

---

[8] BDU's – Battle Dress Uniform, also known as camouflaged fatigues

get hold of a military Chaplain Duty line? Nothing but God! After some conversation I discovered this young man was a drug addict and his wife had left him and taken the children because of his addiction. Now, desperate and hurting he was threatening to end his life. I identified that ending his life was not what he really wanted, but help and hope was what he was looking for. When he told me he lived in the rougher neighborhood of Fayetteville and it was late at night. We made an agreement: If he surrendered the weapon to a family member and got some rest I promised him I would come to his location and help him. He agreed. The following day keeping my word I went to his location. Dressed in uniform I went to a neighborhood location and met the young man. While talking to him about how to get him help for his addiction another man came out of the house in front of his apartment with an AK-47 weapon. The man with the drug addiction began getting extremely nervous as he told me this was the drug dealer he gets his drugs from. I recognized the dealer was threatening me because I was threatening his income. I went to the front of my car facing the drug dealer and sat on the hood. I looked directly into his eyes as if to say, "What are you going to do?" After several tense seconds, the man looked at me took the weapon as if playing with it and turned away going back into the house. With that rebuke of the enemy, the young man who was addicted to drugs got into a rehabilitation program, and was eventually reunited with his family. This again is a testimony of God's goodness and grace. **This is what God can do when you have faith and trust Him.**

## INSPIRATION

I recently attended a Train the Trainer Program that really helped me to see the current needs I have in order to grow and to make more of a significant difference in life. All that has happened to me is because of who I was. All that I will become tomorrow is because of who I choose to be. I choose to be Powerful, Present, and most importantly, to play Big! At the training I realized why I play small, it has to do with being afraid to show myself. I have allowed my injury, my past fears and failures to keep me from running, speaking, and basically sharing who I am. The bottom line is: *I had not accepted myself.* Not only had I not accepted myself *I really didn't like who I was.*

With all the struggles and failures I've experienced in life, and with the traumatic head injury, I gave up on myself. It was only through the faith of my wife, continuous therapy, counseling, prayer, and the involvement of an excellent group of mentors and coaches that I began to get inspired inch-by-inch. For example: when working with the coaches of Build Forward Coaching, they saw in me what God saw in me. They saw the significant message I had to give to the world. They met with me and told me often that what I had to give was important and needed for the world today.

## VICTORY

The key to success is action. When I began to write this book, and when I began to speak I began to feel powerful and significant again. This is not to say I did not have moments where my insecurities came up again. Like when being asked to give a toast for a power couple at a wedding, I bombed. I gave an empty speech that did not speak to them or their moment. That little voice began to speak to me LOUDLY, "...you fool, you messed up again!" I felt my spirit diminish, my presence withdraw. I did all I could do at the moment to keep from completely shutting down. I was hurt, wounded and disappointed with myself from that experience. Who was I fooling? Myself? I wanted to give up in doing all the things I was doing; speaking, writing the book, beginning to dream again! All I wanted to do was to go into the shell. **But I didn't! Why?**

## EXERCISE

What all these struggles and troubles are designed to do are to provide you with opportunities to Exercise your Faith in God. I admit some of our problems and challenges can be bigger than any of us, but with God nothing is impossible! Everything in life comes down to, will I trust Him! That's Satan's biggest desire to get us to doubt God. Jesus said these key words in the Bible that I really think we have a tendency to overlook and minimize:

### Luke 18:7-8 New King James Version (NKJV)

7. And shall God not avenge His own elect who cry out day and night to Him, though He bears long with them?

8. I tell you that He will avenge them speedily. Nevertheless, when the Son of Man comes, will He really **find faith** on the earth?

From the beginning Adam and Eve looked at the Tree of the Knowledge of Good and Evil, and with doubt in God's Word as to who they were, and whose they were, they didn't believe.

That's what life really is about. Can we believe, have faith, and trust God even when all hell breaks loose.

# RETIRED FROM THE MILITARY – REFUELED FOR THE MISSION

# RETIRED FROM THE MILITARY – REFUELED FOR THE MISSION

## Chaplain's Corner
**Capt. Howard J. Busch, Jr.**
**37th Engineer Battalion**

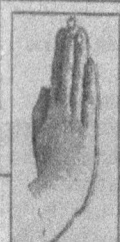

The night of Feb. 1, I hooked up with other paratroopers waiting for the green light. My heart was beating fast with anticipation.

Standing there I prayed a final prayer, thanking God for protecting each and every individual exiting the aircraft.

That's the last thing I remember! I woke up in the hospital, an IV in my arm and hearing the sound of the vital sign monitor.

What had happened? Why was I here? Had not God protected me? I couldn't remember a thing.

During a full month of recuperation, I learned I had a head concussion that completely wiped out my memory of the night's events and left me with some memory complications.

Several individuals told me that I had been in a "mother of all twists." The Parachute Landing Fall could have been fatal when I hit my head. I was instantly knocked unconscious and was bleeding.

Thanks be to God for the outstanding expertise and efforts of the medics who quickly stabilized me and evacuated me to the hospital.

The fascinating thing about this is that I don't remember one thing except standing up at the door waiting for the green light and thanking God for watching over us.

So what did I learn from this experience?

I learned that as soldiers we work in a very high risk occupation that could call for us to give our lives in accomplishing the mission. I also learned the importance of keeping my Chin to Chest ... Chin to Chest ... Chin to Chest.

But most importantly I learned the significance of Psalms 23.

*Even though I walk through the valley of the shadow of death, I will fear no evil for you are with me. Your rod and your staff they comfort me.*

Dynamically important is our relationship with God, He takes care of us no matter what the situation, even if it involves the valley of death.

What has been the end result of this airborne operation for me? When making my next jump I know that my relationship with God gives me peace in any situation.

Secondly, the prayers I have for the soldiers will have a deeper meaning because I know the Lord walks with us in good and bad situations.

And finally I realize the importance of having a good chute and God as my airborne buddy — Airborne!

## Humble Beginnings, Discovering New Beginnings

I learned to S.O.A.R. (Andrea's final Remarks)

As I mentioned in an earlier chapter I learned through my marriage to James and all the different challenges we encountered to **S.O.A.R.** We've overcome much and soar everyday to new heights in our life to experience joy; with the promise of more joy to come. We continue to fight the good fight of faith individually and as a family. We've shared with you our life story. We understand that weeping endures for a night, but JOY does come in the morning. So, if you're in the middle of your weeping (your darkest moment), know that your joy will and is to come; your morning (your bright day) is on its way.

### Psalm 30 New King James Version (NKJV)

1. I will extol You, O LORD, for You have lifted me up, And have not let my foes rejoice over me.

2. O LORD my God, I cried out to You, And you healed me.

3. O LORD, You brought my soul up from the grave; You have kept me alive, that I should not go down to the pit.

4. Sing praise to the LORD, you saints of His, And give thanks at the remembrance of His holy name.

5. For His anger *is but for* a moment, His favor *is* for life; Weeping may endure for a night, But joy *comes* in the morning.

6. Now in my prosperity I said, I shall never be moved.

7. LORD, by Your favor You have made my mountain stand strong; You hid Your face, *and* I was troubled.

8. I cried out to You, O LORD; And to the LORD I made supplication:

9. What profit *is there* in my blood, When I go down to the pit? Will the dust praise You? Will it declare Your truth?

10. Hear, O LORD, and have mercy on me; Lord, be my helper!"

11. You have turned for me my mourning into dancing; You have put off my sackcloth and clothed me with gladness,

12. To the end that *my* glory may sing praise to You and not be silent. O Lord my God, I will give thanks to You forever.

## **S**HIFT

If you're experiencing a dark moment or a prolonged struggle in your life right now, (whatever that is for you), know that it's time to believe your joy has come. In just reflecting back over the different challenges in our life, whether it was financial, marital, or the time when they told us our son's challenge, I have to confess, I cried often. I blamed myself often. At the time, I couldn't understand "why" this young man. He was a very good child growing up. I reflected on the stories that made him such a special and unique child. As I thought on his life more, my perspective on "why him" grew with my sadness and my tears. But after cleansing myself of the tears, I finally realized I could not keep sitting on my couch crying every day without doing something or making a change. Little by little, I begin to shift.

Shift as defined by Webster's is the ability to move or cause (something or someone) to move to a different place, position, etc. The Latin word for 'Shift' is A**move**o, which is to move away from. Noticed the word "**move**" even found in the Latin word.

How was I going to shift to a different place or position in my life? How were we going to get our son / our family to a different place in life than where we were in that moment; our night time of weeping? It was a time to shift.

Have you ever noticed a car with a standard transition; you have to actually shift the gears from one speed to another. It was that sense of changing (like the SHIFT of a gear in a car) that I knew I needed to make. For you non-automatic car lovers, there's usually anywhere from three to five gears to shift your vehicle before riding smoothly on the highway. Having been an experienced driver with gears, I also know that when you are on bumpy roads, hills, and inclines, you can't suddenly shift gears into fifth speed. You can't go from first gear to fifth gear just like that. You progressively go from first to second, second to third and so on. You almost have to have the correct speed to properly shift gears.

## GET OVER IT

As a part of the shifting I had to make, I also had to learn how to get over what happened to our son. James talks about what he learned from the military, I learned through my military service that when I was most challenged in my training, I still had to accomplish the mission. I still had to get to the destination my commanders and/or trainers required me to reach.

I recall being in one of my military field training exercises where, in the middle of a cold wet, rainy night, I was feeling miserable. They had taken our tents away and that night we were to learn how to work with our battle buddy to create a tent with our ponchos. It had been hot earlier in the day but raining, that night it rained even more. My clothes were damp and in the night, under the poncho, I felt physical pain in my body from shivering and being cold throughout the night. From that experience, I knew all too much the reality of the military saying, ***"Suck it up and drive on!"*** The next morning we had to get up and still complete our training mission.

I knew what they were telling me about my son was not the end. I knew I needed to shift and in order to shift I had to get to a point of, "Sucking it up and driving on."

## Take Action

To get over it, to shift, you have to take action. The vehicle will not move without you actually hitting the clutch, moving the gears from one to the other, and then hitting the gas. Action implies doing something.

I couldn't sit on the couch crying every day and night while my son was praying for himself that he wouldn't continue to feel the way he was. It hurt both our hearts to see him and it touched us especially when he said, "Dad, I'm praying."

We had to begin to see him different from what we heard, what we read about his mental illness (personality disorder), and what we saw happen. I had to do something. That shift for me began slowly from one gear to the next. I began to get over what happened and I took action; I purposed to do whatever God required of me.

## RENEW MY MIND

For me that doing something had to begin with my mind. The one scripture that stuck with me while attending Evangel Fellowship in Greensboro, NC was Romans 12.

> **Romans 12:1-2** (NKJV)
>
> 1. I beseech you therefore, brethren, by the mercies of God, that you present your bodies a living sacrifice, holy acceptable to God, which is your reasonable service.
>
> 2. And do not be conformed to this world, but be transformed by the renewing of your mind, that you prove what is that good and acceptable and perfect will of God.

This wasn't about just reading a scripture that sounded good to the ear. It was time for another shift, a transformation in the life of my family; this time my son. I revisited a book I had read before, I bought the child and teen version for my children.

I decided it was time to read/listen to it again and again. While on walks, and rides in the car, it began with listening to the audio book, "Battlefield of the Mind." That was the beginning. Faith comes by hearing and hearing by the Word of God...

James for the last several years had made it a habit of listening to the Word in the car while on long trips, etc. When Joshua graduated from school and started to stabilize, it was not long before I began looking for work again. I wanted to go back to the federal government but hiring was not the best in the federal government at that time. Regardless, I began to apply. I got a break with a federal contracting job when I went into an interview for a different position. However, I was focused to get us back on the road to financial recovery. I went in for the interview and afterwards they told me they already filled the position, but had another position I was better qualified for. When she told me what it was, I praised God for it because it was a supervisory level with a team. As we mentioned in the earlier chapter, I eventually regained my tenure back with the federal government but it was on those rides every day to work together we'd listen to the reaffirmation of God's Word in our life. You see, James chose to drive me into the office on many mornings so we could have some morning time together.

As I renewed my mind, not just one time, not just in a crisis, not just a day here and there, but each day, I began to take action in my life. As I took action, it became easier to get over all that happened; by forgetting those things behind me and pressing toward the mark for a higher calling. As I renewed my mind each day, as I took little and big actions in my life, I would also begin to shift or move my positioning. Sometimes that move of "positioning" may have been just changing my perspective of what hurt or bothered me.

Have you ever seen an eagle soar in the air? It is a beautiful breath taking sight. Therein lies the sight of freedom as you watch an eagle soar. I am more in love with James Busch today than I was yesterday like my grandfather said. Yesterdays are gone and what happened then is gone, it is what we build forward that matters.

All in all, I learned to S.O.A.R. through my life with James, the weeping of nights with our son's challenges; or any challenges we've had for that matter. I, we, our family continue to soar, soar, soar, S.O.A.R. James retired from the military and now he (we) are refueled for the mission.

**Isaiah 40:31** (NKJV)

31. But for those who wait on the Lord shall renew *their* strength;
They shall mount up with wings like eagles,
They shall run and not be weary,
They shall walk and not faint.

# RETIRED FROM THE MILITARY – REFUELED FOR THE MISSION

# RETIRED FROM THE MILITARY – REFUELED FOR THE MISSION

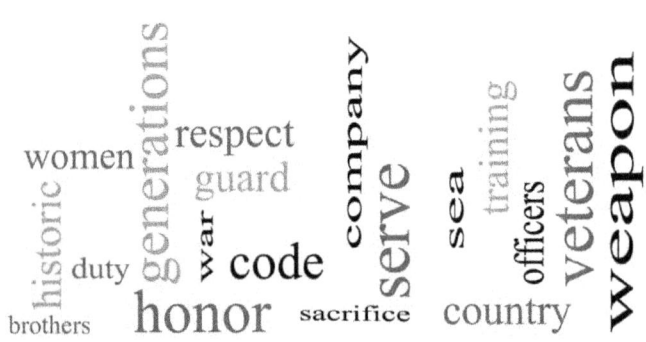

# MILITARY
## RESOURCES AND REFERENCES

This section will assist you in having access to the resources of lessons I learned in the Military.

**2 Timothy 2:4** (NKJV)
**"No man engaged in warfare entangles himself with the affairs of *this* life; that he may please Him who enlisted him to be a soldier."**

Definition of **MILITARY**

**Adjective:**
Relating to or characteristic of soldiers or armed forces

**Noun:**
The armed forces of a country

---

1. **Authority** – Chain of Command
2. **Military Values**
3. **Be, Know and Do**
4. **Staff Organization and Operations** (FM-101-5)
5. **Soldiering** – Training, Perseverance and Duty
6. **Sacrifice** – Willingness to give life for others
7. **Mission** – Fight to Win!

## *Be, Know and Do*

To assist soldiers aspiring to noncommissioned officer ranks, several senior NCO's who recently served on NCO promotion boards and junior non-commissioned officers who have recently competed for promotion collected their insight to offer the following tips. The tips for promotion are organized by the leadership paradigm of **BE-KNOW-DO:**

## **BE**

- Believe in yourself, your mission, your unit, and the United States Army
- Select a role model and follow his or her example
- Find the best in others and emulate their attributes
- Display physical and moral courage; take the initiative and make things happen
- Show commitment; take charge at every opportunity
- Be a coach, leader, mentor, and trainer
- Be honest and truthful; be a person of your word
- Be receptive to constructive criticism
- Maintain a positive mental attitude in every circumstance, but especially when conditions are at their worst
- Do what it takes to get the job done right, but do it in accordance with laws, regulations, and orders
- Approach every problem as a challenge to be overcome and as an opportunity to learn and grow
- Thrive on chaos; be flexible and agile and be ready and willing to adapt to change
- Be decisive; use your judgment and don't be afraid to make a decision

# KNOW

- Earn the reputation as a subject matter expert on your job; know the nuances of your assigned responsibilities better than anyone else in your outfit
- Constantly improve your speaking and writing skills
- Become an expert instructor
- Learn how to motivate groups of soldiers to perform a mission; master team development skills
- Know your equipment, vehicle, and weapons; be an expert on operator level maintenance
- Learn and know the history of our Nation and of our Army
- Stay abreast of current events by reading the newspaper daily
- Take courses or read technical manuals to remain current on the status of Army technology

# DO

- Join a professional association
- Maintain your physical and mental health
- Always arrive early and leave late
- Maintain an impeccable appearance
- Listen, observe, learn, and always ask questions
- Seek a leadership position at the next higher level and do it well
- Volunteer for additional duties
- Pursue a rigorous personal physical training regimen
- Strive to max the Army Physical Fitness Test
- Develop and lead a vigorous training program for your organization
- Improve your marksmanship skills and scores (get your eyes checked annually) and assist your peers and subordinates in improving their marksmanship skills
- Reclassify into a shortage military occupation specialty, if appropriate
- Take CLEP and DANTES tests
- Take action to achieve a GT score of 110 or higher
- Build your military education portfolio by enrolling in correspondence courses

- Take college courses to get a degree; then continue to work on the next higher level degree
- Enhance your professional qualifications; earn the Expert Infantryman's or Medic's Badges or become a Master Fitness Trainer or Combat Lifesaver
- Strive for the tough jobs and do them well; volunteer for Ranger training/assignment, Airborne training/assignment, Drill Sergeant school/assignment, Recruiting course/assignment, or TO&E assignments

# The First Core Value: Integrity First

The Airman is a person of integrity, courage and conviction.

Integrity is a character trait. It is the willingness to do what is right even when no one is looking. It is the moral compass, the inner voice, the voice of self-control and the basis for the trust imperative in today's military.

Integrity is the ability to hold together and properly regulate all of the elements of a personality. A person of integrity, for example, is capable of acting on conviction. A person of integrity can control impulses and appetites.

But integrity also covers several other moral traits indispensable to national service.

### Courage
A person of integrity possesses moral courage and does what is right even if the personal cost is high.

### Honesty
Honesty is the hallmark of the military professional because in the military, our word must be our bond. We don't pencil-whip training reports, we don't cover up tech data violations, we don't falsify documents and we don't write misleading operational readiness messages. The bottom line is: We don't lie, and we can't justify any deviation.

### Responsibility
No person of integrity is irresponsible; a person of true integrity acknowledges his/her duties and acts accordingly.

## Accountability

No person of integrity tries to shift the blame to others or take credit for the work of others. "The buck stops here" says it best.

## Justice

A person of integrity practices justice. Those who do similar things must get similar rewards or similar punishments.

## Openness

Professionals of integrity encourage a free flow of information within the organization. They seek feedback from all directions to ensure they are fulfilling key responsibilities, and they are never afraid to allow anyone at any time to examine how they do business.

## Self-respect

To have integrity is also to respect oneself as a professional and a human being. A person of integrity does not behave in ways that would bring discredit upon himself/herself or the organization to which he/she belongs.

## Humility

A person of integrity grasps and is sobered by the awesome task of defending the Constitution of the United States of America.

# The Second Core Value: Service *Before* Self

An Airman's professional duties always take precedence over personal desires.

Service before self tells us that professional duties take precedence over personal desires. At the very least, it includes the following behaviors:

### Rule following

To serve is to do one's duty, and our duties are most commonly expressed through rules. While it may be the case that professionals are expected to exercise judgment in the performance of their duties, good professionals understand that rules have a reason for being - and the default position must be to follow those rules unless there is a clear, operational reason for refusing to do so.

### Respect for others

Service before self tells us also that a good leader places the troops ahead of his/her personal comfort. We must always act in the certain knowledge that all persons possess a fundamental worth as human beings.

### Discipline and self-control

Professionals cannot indulge themselves in self-pity, discouragement, anger, frustration or defeatism. They have a fundamental moral obligation to the persons they lead to strike a tone of confidence and forward-looking optimism. More specifically, they are expected to exercise control in the following areas:

### Anger

Military professionals and especially commanders at all echelons are expected to refrain from displays of anger that would bring discredit upon themselves and/or the Air Force.

## Appetites

Those who allow their appetites to drive them to make sexual overtures to subordinates are unfit for military service. Likewise, the excessive consumption of alcohol casts doubt on an individual's fitness.

## Religious toleration

Military professionals must remember that religious choice is a matter of individual conscience. Professionals - and especially commanders - must not take it upon themselves to change or coercively influence the religious views of subordinates.

# The Third Core Value: Excellence in All We Do

Every American Airman strives for continual improvement in self and service.

Excellence in all we do directs us to develop a sustained passion for continuous improvement and innovation that will propel the Air Force into a long-term, upward spiral of accomplishment and performance.

### Product/service excellence

We must focus on providing services and generating products that fully respond to customer wants and anticipate customer needs, and we must do so within the boundaries established by the tax-paying public.

### Personal excellence

Military professionals must seek out and complete professional military education, stay in physical and mental shape and continue to refresh their general educational backgrounds.

### Community excellence

Community excellence is achieved when the members of an organization can work together to successfully reach a common goal in an atmosphere that is free from fear and that preserves individual self-worth. Some of the factors influencing interpersonal excellence are:

### Mutual respect

Genuine respect involves viewing another person as an individual of fundamental worth. Obviously, this means that a person is never judged on the basis of his/her possession of an attribute that places him/her in some racial, ethnic, economic or gender-based category.

## Benefit of the doubt

Working hand in glove with mutual respect is that attitude that says all coworkers are innocent until proven guilty. Before rushing to judgment about a person or his/her behavior, it is important to have the whole story.

## Resources excellence

Excellence in all we do also demands that we aggressively implement policies to ensure the best possible cradle-to-grave management of resources.

## Material resources excellence

Military professionals have an obligation to ensure that all of the equipment and property they ask for is mission essential. This means that residual funds at the end of the year should not be used to purchase "nice to have" add-ons.

## Human resources excellence

Human resources excellence means that we recruit, train, promote and retain those who can do the best job for us.

## Operations excellence

There are two kinds of operations excellence: internal and external.

## Excellence of internal operations

This form of excellence pertains to the way we do business internal to the Air Force from the unit level to Air Force Headquarters. It involves respect on the unit level and a total commitment to maximizing the Air Force team effort.

## Excellence of external operations

This form of excellence pertains to the way in which we treat the world around us as we conduct our operations. In peacetime, for example, we must be sensitive to the rules governing environmental pollution, and in wartime we are required to obey the laws of war.

# Warrior Ethos

I will always place the mission first.

I will never accept defeat.

I will never quit.

I will never leave a fallen comrade.

Many people know what the words Loyalty, Duty, Respect, Selfless Service, Honor, Integrity, and Personal Courage mean. But how often do you see someone actually live up to them? Soldiers learn these values in detail during Basic Combat Training (BCT), from then on they live them every day in everything they do – whether they're on the job or off. In short, the Seven Core Army Values listed below are what being a Soldier is all about.

Loyalty
Bear true faith and allegiance to the U.S. Constitution, the Army, your unit and other Soldiers. Bearing true faith and allegiance is a matter of believing in and devoting yourself to something or someone. A loyal Soldier is one who supports the leadership and stands up for fellow Soldiers. By wearing the uniform of the U.S. Army you are expressing your loyalty. And by doing your share, you show your loyalty to your unit.

Duty
Fulfill your obligations. Doing your duty means more than carrying out your assigned tasks. Duty means being able to accomplish tasks as part of a team. The work of the U.S. Army is a complex combination of missions, tasks and responsibilities – all in constant motion. Our work entails building one assignment onto another. You fulfill your obligations as a part of your unit every time you resist the temptation to take "shortcuts" that might undermine the integrity of the final product.

Respect
Treat people as they should be treated. In the Soldier's Code, we pledge to "treat others with dignity and respect while expecting others to do the same." Respect is what allows us to appreciate the best in other people. Respect is trusting that all people have done their jobs and fulfilled their duty. And self-respect is a vital ingredient with the Army value of respect, which results from knowing you have put forth your best effort. The Army is one team and each of us has something to contribute.

RETIRED FROM THE MILITARY – REFUELED FOR THE MISSION

Selfless Service
Put the welfare of the nation, the Army and your subordinates before your own. Selfless service is larger than just one person. In serving your country, you are doing your duty loyally without thought of recognition or gain. The basic building block of selfless service is the commitment of each team member to go a little further, endure a little longer, and look a little closer to see how he or she can add to the effort.

Honor
Live up to Army values. The nation's highest military award is The Medal of Honor. This award goes to Soldiers who make honor a matter of daily living – Soldiers who develop the habit of being honorable, and solidify that habit with every value choice they make. Honor is a matter of carrying out, acting, and living the values of respect, duty, loyalty, selfless service, integrity and personal courage in everything you do.

Integrity
Do what's right, legally and morally. Integrity is a quality you develop by adhering to moral principles. It requires that you do and say nothing that deceives others. As your integrity grows, so does the trust others place in you. The more choices you make based on integrity, the more this highly prized value will affect your relationships with family and friends, and, finally, the fundamental acceptance of yourself.

Personal Courage
Face fear, danger or adversity (physical or moral). Personal courage has long been associated with our Army. With physical courage, it is a matter of enduring physical duress and at times risking personal safety. Facing moral fear or adversity may be a long, slow process of continuing forward on the right path, especially if taking those actions is not popular with others. You can build your personal courage by daily standing up for and acting upon the things that you know are honorable.

## The Unit Chaplain: Roles and Responsibilities

As the spiritual leaders of the military, chaplains are responsible for tending to the spiritual well-being of service members and their families. The chaplain's responsibilities include everything from performing weddings and conducting worship services to providing personal counseling and advising commanders on moral and ethical issues. Unit ministry teams (UMT) in the Army; religious ministry teams (RMT) in the Marine Corps, Navy and Coast Guard; and religious support teams (RST) in the Air Force refer to teams consisting of at least one chaplain and at least one chaplain assistant (in the Army and Air Force) or religious program specialist (in the Marine Corps, Navy or Coast Guard). These teams perform a variety of functions to support the chaplain. Chaplains are commissioned officers, and chaplain assistants and religious program specialists are enlisted personnel.

Your chaplain's first obligations are to active duty service members and their family members. These obligations include the following:

- **Conducting worship and administering sacraments** — Chaplains are responsible for making sure that service members have the opportunity to worship as they choose. This means that chaplains conduct worship services and administer sacraments consistent with their own faith and also seek out accommodations for persons of other faiths. For example, since a Protestant chaplain can't legitimately perform a Mass for Roman Catholics, the chaplain can locate a Roman Catholic chaplain to administer the sacrament.

- **Performing other religious ceremonies and services** — Chaplains also perform religious rites and ceremonies such as marriages and funeral or memorial services.

- **Counseling service members and their families** — While chaplains are not generally licensed counselors, they are often called on to help people with various life challenges— including issues related to combat stress, deployment, marriage, profession, family, substance abuse and finances.

However, many of them do have expertise in premarital counseling and grief counseling. These types of counseling situations fall under the heading of "pastoral care." Although chaplains are expected to be knowledgeable about the basics of various personal issues, they are also expected to be able to refer individuals to other counseling sources when they do not feel qualified or cannot counsel for some other reason. All communications with a chaplain, chaplain assistant or religious program specialist are confidential. These communications cannot be disclosed to anyone else without the permission of the person seeking counseling.

- **Visitation** — Through visitation to injured or sick service members (at home or in the hospital) chaplains offer comfort, spiritual support and pastoral care to those dealing with illness or injury.

- **Advising commanders on moral, ethical and spiritual issues** — Chaplains serve as advisors to commanders on all matters of morality, integrity and religion, which may include the following:
    - meeting the religious needs of assigned personnel
    - assessing the spiritual, ethical and moral climate of the command
    - planning and programming related to the moral and ethical quality of leadership, the care of people, religious education and related funding issues associated with religious programming within the command
    - overseeing the construction of religious facilities
    - publicizing religious program activities

- **Developing religious education programs and youth activities** — At the installation, the chaplain provides religious instruction and is responsible to the commander for religious education programs such as Sunday school classes and youth programs. They also train lay leaders who conduct religious education programs. Lay leaders are trained volunteers appointed by the installation chaplain to meet the needs of a particular religious faith group when military chaplains of that faith group are not available. Lay leaders operate with the written approval of their faith group and under the supervision of the service chaplaincy.

- **Conducting seminars and retreats** — Chaplains conduct seminars and retreats for the moral, spiritual and social development of service members and their families. Seminar topics may include the following:

  - marriage enrichment
  - parenting skills
  - spiritual leadership training
  - service member transition from combat operation
  - anger management
  - spiritual formation for youth and adults

- **Instructing chaplains and chaplain assistants** — Your installation chaplain plans, conducts, assesses, monitors and supports the training of all subordinate chaplains, as well as chaplain assistants or religious program specialists.

- **Accompanying service members into combat** — Chaplains must be willing to go where needed and this includes combat situations with service members. The chaplain is a noncombatant and carries no weapon. The chaplain assistant or religious program specialist is a combatant and ensures force protection for the chaplain in hostile environments.

- **Combat stress intervention** — By implementing a comprehensive operational stress control ministry, the chaplain team forms an important component of the commander's program of stress control. This team provides immediate support to leaders in fulfilling their stress identification and intervention responsibilities. The team also helps train leaders in the chain of command to recognize stress symptoms and trains others in basic counseling skills to enable service members to communicate their stress. Chaplains work very closely with military medical personnel in training and treatment related to this important issue.

# SPIRITUAL
## Resources and References

# My Life Statement

## I am an Ambassador for the Kingdom of God:

•   My mission is to abide in Jesus Christ in order to be an expression of Jesus Christ in the earth, and to glorify God with my life.

•   My motivation is that, " I can do all things through Christ who strengthens me. "

•   My message is that you cannot get to the promise unless you are willing to go through the process. Every test is for the purpose of providing you a testimony.

*Given by* **H. James Busch, Jr.**

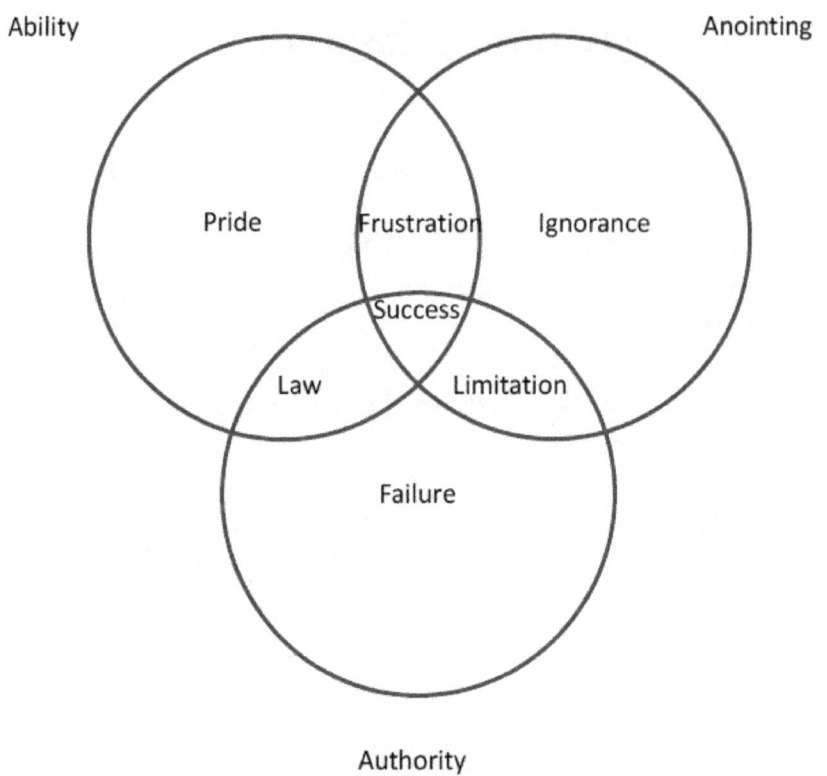

Ability without Anointing = Pride
Anointing without Ability = Ignorance
Ability + Anointing without Authority = Frustration
Authority + Ability without Anointing = Law
Authority without Ability = Failure
Authority + Anointing without Ability = Limitation
Authority + Ability + Anointing = Success

*Given in Eldership Training by* **Bishop Gary McIntosh**

WriteHouse is a Full Service Publishing Company;
*We make YOUR goal to publish DOABLE.*

www.writehousepublishing.com

202.714.7724

# REFUELED for the MISSION
# ALL to the GLORY of GOD

www.ingramcontent.com/pod-product-compliance
Lightning Source LLC
Chambersburg PA
CBHW070812100426
42742CB00012B/2336